In memory of
Oro Sultani Benaroya
and
Isaac Benaroya

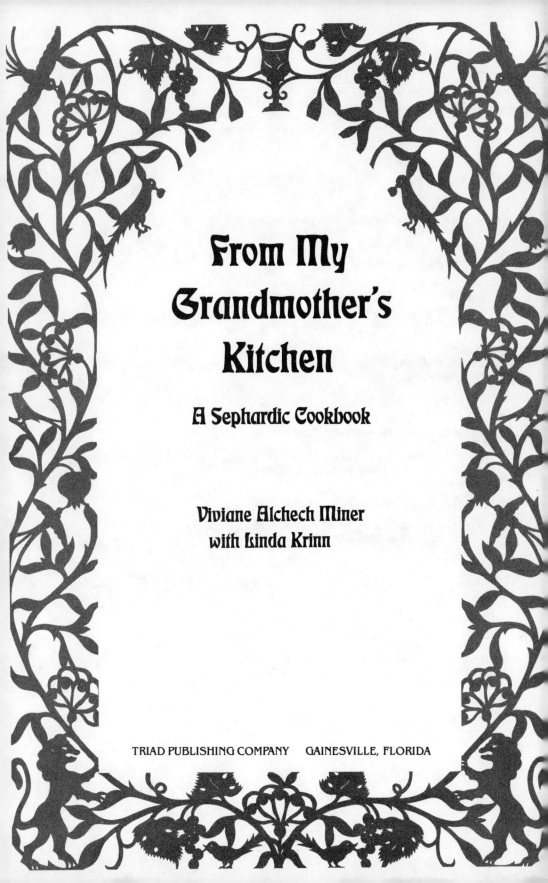

From My Grandmother's Kitchen

A Sephardic Cookbook

Viviane Alchech Miner
with Linda Krinn

TRIAD PUBLISHING COMPANY   GAINESVILLE, FLORIDA

Library of Congress Cataloging in Publication Data

Miner, Viviane, 1945-
  From my grandmother's kitchen.

  Includes index.
1. Cookery, Jewish. 2. Sephardim — Switzerland —
Geneva — Social life and customs. 3. Geneva
(Switzerland) — Social life and customs. I. Krinn,
Linda, 1942-
II. Title.
TX724.M56 1984   641.5'676   84-8885
ISBN 0-937404-23-3 (pbk).

Printed in the United States of America

Published and distributed by Triad Publishing
Company, Inc. 1110 NW 8th Avenue, Gainesville,
Florida 32601

From my Grandmother's Kitchen is available at
special quantity discounts for bulk purchases for sales
promotion, premiums, or fund raising. For details
write the Director of Special Sales, Triad Publishing
Company, 1110 Northwest Eighth Avenue, Gainesville,
Florida 32601.

I dedicate this book to all my friends,
as well as the families —
Sultani
  Benaroya   Alchech
    Vaëna   Finzi
      Pinhas   Naftule
        Behar   Henriot
          Gerson   Vaëssa
            Delarena   Mizrachi

without whom all the memories, pictures,
and recipes would not have been possible,
and especially to my mother, who is the best.

ABOUT THE AUTHORS

Viviane Alchech Miner is a descendant of two distinguished Sephardic families. She inherited the wealth of recipes that make up this book from her mother's family, the Benaroyas. Until the age of nine, Viviane lived in Switzerland amidst the large and closely knit Benaroya family, who had been an influential part of the Sephardic community in Geneva since the turn of the century. Her fondest memories are of helping her grandparents cook.

On her father's side, Viviane is a member of the Alchech family, descendents of a long line of rabbinical and Talmudic commentators and Kabalists that extends as far back as the 1600s.

Viviane's family came to America in 1954. Today she is a graphic designer who lives with her husband and children in Rockville, Maryland. She continues cooking in the Sephardic tradition for family and friends.

Linda Krinn is a writer who lives in Bethesda, Maryland.

ABOUT THE COVER

The original paper-cut design is by Tamar Fishman, an Israeli-born artist living in Bethesda, Maryland.

Jewish paper-cuts were a form of folk art popular with Jews of Poland and Russia in the late 19th and early 20th century. Paper-cuts with an oriental style were also found among Jews in North Africa and the Middle East. The designs were hung on the eastern wall of synagogues and homes to indicate the direction of prayer and were used for a variety of decorative purposes as well. In recent years, Jewish artisans have revived the art of paper-cutting.

Tamar Fishman's paper-cut for the cover of *From My Grandmother's Kitchen* incorporates a number of Jewish symbols. The pomegranate is a symbol of abundance, of fertility and of life itself. The lion, one of the most frequently mentioned animals in the Bible, represents the Lion of Judah. Grapes and the wine cup are symbols of sanctification, and the birds suggest freedom.

Contents

Recipe Contents

Chicken

Rice, Beans and Noodles

Vegetables

Savory Pastries

Tarts, Pies and Pastries

Fruit and Other Desserts

Cookies

Cakes

From My
Grandmother's
Kitchen

My grandmother Oro Sultani, her brother Mordi, and their parents. 1905.

Isaac and Perla Pinhas, Oro and Isaac Benaroya. Marseille, circa 1928.

*My grandmother Oro Sultani and two
of her oldest sisters.*

Geneva, 1905.

*Grandmother Oro's mother,
Fortané Sultani.*

Introduction

I come from a long line of Sephardic Jews. *Sepharad* means "Spain" in Hebrew and traditionally refers to the descendants of Spanish and Portuguese Jews who fled Iberia in the fifteenth century to escape the Inquisition. Over the years, however, the word *Sephardic* has become all-embracing. Many people connect the word to anything Mediterranean or they use the term to include all Jews who do not trace their ancestry to northern Europe. Some Jews are labeled Sephardic because of their culture or customs. But three characteristics unite all Sephardim: pride in their heritage, a love of Judaism, and a long tradition of hospitality.

My ancestors left the province of Murcia, Spain, in 1425. They sailed eastward to countries that were then part of the vast Ottoman Empire — Bulgaria, Yugoslavia, Greece, Romania and other countries ringing the eastern Mediterranean. Salonika, now in Greece, became the intellectual and cultural center for the Sephardic Jews of the European Ottoman Empire. United by their religion, customs, trade, and even their own language, Ladino, these self-contained communities flourished until the convulsions of the twentieth century disrupted and destroyed them.

Through the centuries, in response to political conditions, persecution, and economic opportunities, Sephardic Jews migrated far and wide. In addition to settling in the Balkans, they made homes in North Africa, the Near East, Italy, France, Holland, Germany and England as well as in North, Central, and South America. A branch of my family settled in Geneva, Switzerland, after leaving the Balkans at the beginning of the twentieth century.

As each group of Sephardim became integrated into a new region, they began using the local fruit and vegetables and adopting cooking techniques that were new to them. They often changed ingredients in ethnic dishes in order to adhere to Jewish dietary laws or to find an outlet for their creativity. As generation after generation modified the indigenous cuisine, a distinctive style of cooking evolved that came to be called Sephardic.

My own family sustained a lively approach to cooking that resulted in a rich legacy of recipes. But nothing was ever written down. The children learned by watching and doing, and they learned at an early age. Everyone in the family considered cooking a privilege, not a chore.

I started watching my grandparents cook when I was five years old. By that time the family was living in Switzerland, where I grew up. I was drawn by the constant hum and gaity in the kitchen — there was always something cooking. The ability to create delicacies from a few ingredients and spices amazed me, especially since it seemed so effortless. My grandparents could slice, chop, mix and taste, all the while chatting with each other and with relatives who came to help out.

I didn't realize until I was older that the food reflected the places where my ancestors had lived, though I remember wondering why our food — the bulemas, borekas, fritadas, and huevos haminadas — was different from that which most of our Swiss friends and neighbors ate.

Finally I asked my grandmother and discovered that our meals were an exotic blend of Turkish, Greek, Bulgarian and Romanian food — with a Spanish influence. My family had transported much of the Sephardic way of life to Geneva, and our cooking was part of that heritage and a connection to a bygone era.

My memories of growing up in Switzerland amid my large gregarious family who loved to cook and eat inspired me to write this cookbook. When my maternal grandmother, Oro Sultani Benaroya, died in 1976 at the age of 85, I realized that there would soon be no one left who could help me record the recipes.

I began by writing down all the family recipes that I knew and used and by asking my brother to do the same. As far as we knew, this was the first time any of these recipes had been written. Then I went to my mother to work out details that I was unsure of and to ask about other recipes that were vague memories in my mind. At first my mother hesitated. It was difficult for her to put years of cooking — seemingly by instinct — into measured formulas. But the key to winning my mother's cooperation turned out to be her own fondness for storytelling. I discovered that the way to get information from her was to evoke memories, so that she would start talking about specific times and holidays. Soon she would be remininscing her way through a loaf of Bulgarian filled bread or a dish of berenjena turquese.

Finally, in August of 1983, I went to Switzerland to talk to the relatives who had been the closest to my grandmother, her children, nieces, nephews and cousins, now in their 70s. They too found it difficult to reduce centuries of cooking into words. Their knowledge is in their fingertips. So we cooked. For over a month, I revisited my childhood, once again learning by doing, and becoming a part of that glorious kitchen warmth and chatter that was my grandmother's kitchen.

Had I waited too long before starting the cookbook, this legacy would surely have been lost. Here, I've recorded the recipes and culinary lore of the Sultani-Benaroya family so that others can enjoy this festive, comforting food. I wanted to preserve what was, for me, the most tangible aspect of the Sephardic way of life, the distinctive food created by generations of Sephardic Jews who lived in the Balkan countries.

VIVIANE MINER
SEPTEMBER 1984

My mother and father's wedding at the Bykour Houlym Synagogue. Geneva, May 22, 1943. Double wedding with her cousins Joseph Sultani and Chorine Vaëssa (who also went with them on their honeymoon).

Boy scouts from the Maison Juive. Geneva, circa 1922. My father is second from the left.

Sultani and Benaroya cousins in front of the Bykour Houlym Sephardic Synagogue.

Reminiscing

On Geneva's winter evenings, when the snow stood in puffy mounds outside, Grandfather Isaac Benaroya, my mother's father, would light a pile of logs in the fireplace, make a pot of hot chocolate, and gather his grandchildren around. He'd tell us Bible stories and funny anecdotes about our parents. But the real reason for these sessions was to link us to our past by telling us about our forebears, so that we would be proud to be Sephardic Jews.

First, Grandfather would sing ancient folk songs, handed down for generations. One song warned Jews to pack their belongings and flee Spain as soon as their names appeared on a list in the town center. As he sang, we felt the apprehension our ancestors must have felt during the Inquisition so many centuries ago.

Grandfather sang his songs in Judeo-Spanish — now often called Judezmo — a language spoken by all Sephardim. Actually a fifteenth century Castillian with additions of Hebrew and Balkan words, this language was cherished by my family; they even made a distinction between it and Ladino, a mixture of Spanish and Hebrew, which they used for prayer or literary writing.

To cheer us after this song, Grandfather would tell the story about how he and other members of our migrating family settled in Geneva. Grandfather and his brother Eliezer left Varna, Bulgaria at the turn of the century and traveled throughout Turkey. Eventually, they found jobs on shipping lines that sailed between Salonika and Greece. Grandfather, a glass cutter by trade, worked as a cook.

Using his hands in remarkably realistic gestures, Grandfather demonstrated how he made hundreds of apple dumplings for the ship's passengers. He pretended to knead and cut the dough, fill it with apples, then shove the baking pans into the oven. His flying hands and serious expression made us giggle. Grandfather loved to cook, and it was on the ship that he acquired his skill.

On one voyage, Grandfather met an American couple who offered to help him and Eliezer get to the United States. The Americans told the brothers to meet them in Marseille to make the arrangements. Marseille was a major embarkation point for immigrants sailing for America. While in Marseille, Grandfather and his brother made a new friend, a man name Mordi Sultani, who lived in Geneva, Switzerland, and who invited them to visit his home. By coincidence, my grandfather's oldest brother and two of his sisters also lived in Geneva, and he had planned to go there to say goodbye before leaving for America. So, Grandfather and Uncle Eliezer went to see the family and to visit Mordi Sultani.

Then, in spite of his plans to go to America, Grandfather stayed in Geneva because Mordi Sultani introduced him to his sister, Oro, and Grandfather fell in love. My grandparents were formally introduced in 1907 and, after arrangements were made, they married a short time later. My grandmother was 16. My grandparents began working immediately at le marché, the outdoor market.

The family of my grandmother Oro Sultani Benaroya had left Constanza, Romania, when she was very small. They took as many belongings as would fit into a horse-drawn cart and traveled to Turkey where they lived before moving again, this time to Greece. Eventually, they too went to Marseille and from there took a tour to Geneva. They found the city so delightful that they decided to make their home there. It was 1900.

Joseph, Grandfather's oldest brother, had come to Geneva from the Balkans in 1895, bringing his wife, children, and two sisters with him. Joseph had insisted that Pere Issac Vaëna, his brother-in-law-and his family come too. Pere Vaëna was a very religious man who brought with him two Torahs, the handwritten scrolls of the first five books of the Bible. He and Joseph started the Sephardic community in Geneva. Soon after, my great uncle Isaac Pinhas arrived in Geneva with his wife, my grandmother's sister Perla. Issac became president of the congregation, a role he had for 20 years, until a rabbi arrived.

One oral history lesson taught me that marriages in our family had been arranged for centuries. The purpose of this custom was to maintain social and religious traditions and family ties. Grandfather explained that the parents of a prospective couple would sit down together at a table laden with sweet jams, cakes, wine, and Turkish coffee. Each family reported the various household goods, money, or property that would be given to the married couple. If this dowry were satisfactory, the wedding took place within three months. My aunt and uncle Mico and Mica Behar, my aunt and uncle Joseph and Chorine Sultani, and even my mother and father had their marriages arranged.

Girls married at 16 and boys at 18, but once in a while a young girl married a man who was 20 years older than she. This only occurred, Grandfather said, when the girl was very beautiful and the man very rich. A girl who reached the age of 21 without marrying was considered a spinster.

I also learned about an unusual custom concerning a childless couple. If, after many years, a couple failed to conceive a child, a sister or a brother's wife would bestow their next baby to the childless couple who would bring up the child as their own. Indeed, my Aunt Perla and Uncle Isaac Pinhas received a daughter from one of Perla's sisters. Rearing children, I discovered, was considered essential for the happiness of a married couple.

Grandfather told us about the custom of *aliko bini,* which involved taking a child to a relative's house for a few hours while the child's parents were busy with important family obligations. When the child arrived, the aunts and uncles said that he or she had come to get *aliko bini.* The child was swept into their arms and covered with hugs and kisses and then given something to drink and a sweet cake to eat.

Grandfather inspired a sense of religious duty by teaching us that Sephardim, although they immigrated far and wide, clung to their religious traditions; he expected the same steadfastness from us. He told us that there had been no synagogue when our family first arrived in Geneva. The family held services in a small room in one of their apartments and later, when more relatives arrived, they moved to a larger room. When there were too many to fit into the larger room they began sharing a building — called the Maison Juive — with a small Ashkenazi congregation. Ashkenazi refers to Jews from central and northeastern Europe. Grandfather was pleased that he finally had a permanent place to study and discuss the Talmud (rabbinic teachings) and Kabalah (the Jewish mystical tradition).

In the early 1920s the Sephardic congregation built a small synagogue at the Place de la Synagogue on the Rue du Rhone, outside the walls enclosing the city. They named it Group Fraternel Sepharadi Bikour Houlym. Pere Vaëna's Torahs were placed in the lovely new synagogue. Prayers were recited in Hebrew, Ladino, and Aramaic. In 1925 a Sephardic rabbi settled in Geneva and took over the job of leading the congregation, a duty that had been shared until then.

Over the years, the expanding city surrounded the synagogue. Although it was replaced at the end of the 1950s with a larger synagogue, the old one is still used for weddings and other celebrations.

Another need of the growing Sephardic community was a cemetery. Grandfather said that our family donated the money to buy the land, and a site was chosen on the border between France and Switzerland in the town of Veyrier. One entrance was placed directly inside the border of France, so that visitors could reach the cemetery easily from both sides.

Whenever Grandfather grew weary of talking, my mother would take over. She too was an enthusiastic storyteller. One evening she proudly informed us that the Alchechs, my father's family, had produced illustrious scholars and rabbis for 800 years. My parental grandfather, Leon, however, and his eight brothers had apparently refused to carry on the tradition. Furious, Leon's father banished all his sons from Jerusalem. Leon's brothers went to Mexico, America, Germany, and several other countries. But Leon settled in Geneva, coming by way of Milan where he met his wife, Mathilde Finzi of Ferrara.

One story that Mother told made her melancholy, but she insisted on telling it many times. It was about the French Jews during World War II. Most of her friends had relatives living in France. She recalled that everyone was frightened by reports that food was scarce, medicine in short supply, and business collapsing under Nazi pressure.

At once, the young members of the community began taking food and medicine into France by truck. But suddenly the borders closed, and then there were reports that entire communities were disappearing. So the young people waited for the stormiest nights when no one else dared venture out. Bravely crossing the mountains into France on foot, they brought back to Switzerland as many people as they could.

The French Jews and their rescuers were hustled to warm houses where, famished, they feasted on soups and stews served from steaming kettles. They told their harrowing stories and spoke of their plan to hide in Switzerland or to leave immediately for other countries.

The following foods are typical of our hearty winter meals.

Lentil Soup

1/4 cup olive oil
2 large onions, coarsely chopped
2 pounds beef stew, sliced
2 or 3 carrots, sliced
2 or 3 celery stalks with leaves, sliced
4 ripe medium tomatoes
1 quart tomato juice
1 pound brown or red lentils
5 cloves garlic, minced
2 Turkish laurel or bay leaves
1 cup finely chopped parsley
1 teaspoon cumin
1 teaspoon coriander
1/2 teaspoon cinnamon
1 teaspoon saffron
1 teaspoon each salt and pepper, or to taste
1/3 cup vinegar (more if a piquant soup is desired)

Wash lentils and soak for 1 hour in 1 quart boiling water.

In a soup pot, sauté onions and meat in olive oil until the onions are translucent; add carrots and celery, and continue to cook; add tomatoes and sauté a few minutes more. Add tomato juice and 1 quart water and bring to a boil, then add lentils and their soaking liquid, and seasonings.

Cover and simmer for 2 hours until the lentils are tender, adding more water if necessary. Add vinegar during the last 10 minutes of cooking. Taste to correct seasoning.

Serves 8 to 10.

Variation: Substitute a 2 1/2 pound chicken cut in serving pieces for the beef.

Vegetable Soup

6 meaty soup bones, with marrow
3 quarts water
1 pound beef stew meat, cut in bite-size chunks
1/4 cup olive oil
2 medium onions, sliced lengthwise to form crescents
5 cloves garlic, finely chopped
1/2 cup tomato paste
4 carrots, peeled and sliced in rounds
4 celery stalks with leaves, sliced
4 parsnips, peeled and sliced
4 ripe tomatoes, cut into wedges
2 Turkish laurel or bay leaves
Salt and pepper to taste
1 bunch scallions, finely chopped

Place soup bones in a pot, add water, and bring to a boil, skimming foam as it forms. Simmer for 3 hours; remove surface fat.

In a large soup pot, sauté onions, garlic, and meat in olive oil. Add tomato paste and stir. Cook for several minutes. Add the soup bones and broth. Bring to a boil and add all the vegetables (except scallions) and seasonings. Cover and simmer until the vegetables are tender. Add scallions during the last 10 minutes of cooking.

Serves 8 to 10.

Variations: 1 Purée finished soup in a food mill, blender, or food processor; serve with toasted bread spread with olive oil and finely chopped garlic. 2. Add 1 cup cooked pearl barley with the vegetables.

Fidello (Turkish Fried Noodles)

12 ounces vermicelli (very fine noodles), crushed
1/3 olive oil
1 ripe tomato, chopped (optional)
2 1/4 cups beef or chicken stock
Salt and pepper to taste

Heat oil in a frying pan. Add noodles and stir on high heat until noodles are golden. Add tomato, beef stock, salt and pepper. Lower heat and cook uncovered, stirring, until stock is completely absorbed. Serve hot.

Serves 4 to 6.

Bone Marrow Soup

5 ripe tomatoes, peeled
1 bunch leeks
6 tablespoons olive oil or vegetable oil
2 medium onions, chopped
3 carrots, peeled and sliced
1 small celery root (celeriac), sliced
8 ounces vermicelli noodles
2 1/2 quarts water
1 teaspoon salt
1 pound beef marrow bones
1 pound beef bones with meat attached
Salt and pepper to taste

Puree tomatoes in food mill or blender. Cut off roots from bulb end of leeks. Remove tough outer leaves and trim the tips. Slice lengthwise and wash thoroughly under running water. Cut up.

In a soup pot, sauté noodles in 2 tablespoons oil until golden brown; remove. Add 4 tablespoons oil and sauté onions until soft. Stir in carrots and celery root; cook 5 minutes. Add the tomatoes and cook, stirring constantly, for 2 minutes. Add leeks, noodles, water, 1 teaspoon salt, marrow bones, and meat bones; cover and simmer for about 1 hour. Add salt and pepper to taste.

Ladle into soup bowls with 1 or 2 marrow bones in each bowl. Serve with hot bread. Diners will spread marrow on bread and sprinkle with salt and pepper.

Serves 8.

Turkish Rice

1 cup raw rice
1/3 cup olive oil or sesame oil
3 medium onions, sliced lengthwise to form crescents
3 medium green tomatoes, cut into wedges
3 green, yellow, or red peppers, cut into strips
2 1/2 cups boiling water
1 teaspoon salt

Sauté rice in hot olive oil until golden. Stir in vegetables and sauté for 2 minutes. Add water and salt. Stir. Cover and cook on low heat (stirring once after 20 minutes) until water is absorbed, about 45 minutes.

Serves 4.

Dill Chicken Soup

1 soup chicken, cut up
1/4 cup olive oil
3 large onions, sliced in thin wedges
3 carrots, peeled and sliced
Carrot greens, chopped
2 parsnips, peeled and sliced
1 bunch parsley, finely chopped
4 stalks celery with leaves, sliced
1 to 2 teaspoons chopped garlic
2 Turkish laurel or bay leaves
1 bunch scallions, chopped
1/2 cup finely chopped dill weed
Salt and pepper to taste

Place chicken in a large kettle, adding water to cover. Bring to a boil and remove surface foam.

Heat oil and sauté all remaining ingredients except scallions and dill; add to chicken. Add water to cover. Cover pot and simmer until chicken and vegetables are tender. Add scallions and dill during the last 5 minutes of cooking. Add salt and pepper to taste.

Serves 6.

Rice with Scallions and Cheese

3 medium onions, chopped
2 tablespoons olive oil
1 cup raw rice
1 red bell pepper, chopped
Salt and pepper to taste
2 1/2 cups water
1 bunch scallions, chopped
1 cup kaseri or Swiss cheese

Sauté onion in olive oil until soft. Add rice and stir until well coated with oil and slightly colored. Add bell pepper, salt, pepper, and water. Stir to blend. Cover and cook until rice is tender. Add scallions and cheese, mix, and serve hot.

Serves 4 to 6.

Chicken Barley Soup

2 1/2 to 3 pound chicken
2 onions, sliced lengthwise to form crescents
2 cloves garlic, minced
1/4 cup olive oil
1/2 cup pearl barley
Salt and pepper to taste
1/2 cup finely chopped parsley
2 egg yolks, beaten

Remove skin and bones from chicken. Place skin and bones in a large pot with giblets (except the liver) and 1 1/2 quarts water. Simmer for 1 hour, skimming the surface fat. Cook barley in 1 quart water for 1 hour. Cut the chicken meat into very thin pieces about 1 inch long.

In a soup pot, sauté onions and garlic in olive oil until the onions are translucent. Add chicken and cook until it loses its raw color.

When the stock is done, strain and add to the chicken and onions. Drain barley and add to the soup. Cover and simmer for 50 minutes or until the barley is tender. Add salt, pepper, and parsley. Slowly stir in beaten egg yolks. Serve hot with lemon wedges and mint on the side.

Serves 4 to 6.

Rice with Onions and Pine Nuts

2 1/3 cups chicken stock
1 cup raw rice
2 tablespoons pine nuts
2 teaspoons oil
1 large onion, finely chopped
Salt to taste

Bring stock to a boil. Add rice; lower heat and cook until the rice is tender.

Sauté pine nuts in oil until golden; remove from pan. Sauté onion until brown, and remove. Stir nuts and onions into rice with a fork just before serving. Season with salt to taste.

Serves 4 to 6.

Chicken and Pea Soup

1 pound dried green split peas
1/4 cup olive oil
2 onions, finely chopped
5 cloves garlic, minced
2 1/2 pound chicken, cut into serving pieces
2 carrots, peeled and sliced
2 celery stalks with leaves, sliced
2 quarts water
3 Turkish laurel or bay leaves
Salt and pepper to taste
Fresh dill weed, finely chopped

Wash split peas and soak overnight.
In a soup pot, sauté onions, garlic, and chicken in olive oil for 10 minutes, turning chicken to brown on all sides. Stir in carrots and celery and cook 5 minutes. Add remaining ingredients (except dill). Cover and simmer until peas and chicken are tender, about 1 hour. Skim fat from surface of soup. Add dill and serve hot.
Serves 4 to 6.

Rice Cakes

1 onion, chopped
2 cups cooked rice
2 large eggs, beaten
2 tablespoons flour
1/4 cup finely chopped parsley
1/4 cup chopped dill weed
1 cup coarsely grated kaseri or Swiss cheese
Salt and pepper to taste
1/8 teaspoon nutmeg
Oil for frying

Sauté onion lightly in oil. Combine remaining ingredients and mix well. Drop by dollops into hot oil in a large frying pan. Flatten into pancakes and fry on both sides until golden. Do not crowd. Serve hot as a side dish.
Makes 1 dozen.

Cabbage Stew

1 1/4 pounds smoked turkey, cut into small pieces
3 medium onions, sliced lengthwise to form crescents
1/4 cup olive oil
1 pound shredded cabbage
1 tablespoon chopped garlic
1 teaspoon salt
1/2 teaspoon pepper
4 ripe tomatoes, cut into wedges
1/2 cup red wine vinegar
1 cup tomato sauce

In a large soup pot, sauté turkey and onions in olive oil until the onions are soft. Add remaining ingredients and water to cover; stir well. Lower heat to medium; cover and cook gently until the cabbage is tender, about 20 minutes. Stir occasionally.

Taste about halfway through cooking time; if flavor is not piquant enough, add more vinegar. Serve hot in soup bowls with hot bread.

Serves 6.

Rice with Raisins and Pine Nuts

1 large onion, finely chopped
4 tablespoons oil
1 tablespoon pine nuts
1 cup raw rice
2 tablespoons raisins or currants
1/2 teaspoon sugar
1/2 teaspoon cinnamon
1 teaspoon each salt and pepper
1/4 to 1/2 pound chicken livers, broiled and cut into very small pieces
2 1/2 cups boiling water

Sauté onions in oil until golden. Add pine nuts and cook until nuts turn light brown. Remove onions and nuts. In the same pan, sauté the rice, stirring constantly until it becomes golden brown, about 10 minutes. Stir in the onions, pine nuts, and remaining ingredients. Stir well, cover, and cook on low heat until water is absorbed.

Serves 4.

Chick Pea Soup

1 pound dried chick peas
1/4 cup olive oil
3 onions, sliced lengthwise to form crescents
3 teaspoons minced garlic
2 1/2 to 3 pound chicken, cut into serving pieces
3 carrots, sliced
3 celery stalks with leaves, chopped
Salt to taste
1 Turkish laurel or bay leaf
1 quart water

Cover chick peas with 2 quarts water and soak overnight or boil for 30 minutes. Drain, reserving liquid.

In a soup pot, sauté onions and garlic in olive oil. Add chicken, carrots, celery, and salt; cook, stirring, until chicken loses its raw color. Add chick pea liquid, bay leaf, and water; cover and cook until the chicken is tender. Remove chicken and vegetables and set aside. Bone chicken when cool.

Add chick peas to the stock, adding water if necessary to barely cover, and simmer for about 2 hours or until tender. Purée half the soup in a blender or food mill and return to the pot. Add the reserved vegetables and chicken. Simmer for 15 minutes. Serve hot with lemon wedges, fresh chopped dill weed, and cumin powder on the side.

Serves 8 to 10.

Lentils

1 cup lentils
1 large onion, sliced lengthwise into crescents
2 tablespoons olive oil or vegetable oil
2 ripe tomatoes, peeled and chopped
3 cups water
1 tablespoon chopped garlic
Salt and pepper to taste

Soak lentils in boiling water for 1 hour. Sauté onions in olive oil until tender. Add tomatoes and garlic and cook a few more minutes. Add water, lentils, salt and pepper. Cover and simmer for 45 minutes or until lentils are tender and liquid is almost absorbed.

Serves 6.

Green Lemon Soup

3 large leeks
1/4 cup olive oil
2 medium onions, sliced lengthwise to form thin crescents
5 celery stalks with leaves, thinly sliced
3 cloves garlic, finely chopped
2 quarts clear chicken stock
Juice of 1 or 2 lemons, or more to taste
1 1/2 cups cooked white rice
4 pickling cucumbers, peeled and sliced thin
Salt and pepper to taste
1/4 cup chopped dill weed

Cut off roots from bulb end of leeks. Remove tough outer leaves and trim tops. Slice lengthwise and wash thoroughly under cold running water. Slice thin.

In a soup pot, sauté onions in olive oil until translucent. Add celery, leeks, and garlic and sauté a few minutes. Add stock, bring to a boil, and simmer until the vegetables are almost tender. Add lemon juice and rice; simmer 5 minutes. Add cucumber, salt and pepper, and simmer 5 to 10 minutes. Sprinkle with fresh dill weed and serve hot.

Serves 6 to 8.

Polenta with Onions and Cheese

1 large onion, chopped
4 cups water
1 teaspoon salt
1 cup yellow corn meal
1 cup kaseri or Swiss cheese, grated

Sauté onion and set aside.

Combine water and salt and bring to a boil. Lower heat to medium and slowly add corn meal to the boiling water, stirring constantly. Continue to stir until corn meal is cooked. Add cheese and sautéed onions. Serve immediately in warm bowls.

Serves 6.

Variation: Add 3 eggs and bake in well-greased muffin pans at 350° for 25 to 30 minutes.

Tomato Noodle Soup

1/4 cup olive oil
2 medium onions, sliced lengthwise to form thin crescents
2 teaspoons finely chopped garlic
8 ounces vermicelli (fine egg noodles)
5 ripe tomatoes, cut into thin wedges
8 cups beef stock (see Vegetable Soup)
1/2 cup finely chopped parsley
Salt and pepper to taste

In a soup pot, sauté onions in olive oil until translucent. Add garlic and cook about 1 minute, stirring so that it doesn't burn. Crush the noodles with your fingertips and add them to the onions. Cook about 4 minutes or until the noodles turn golden. Add tomatoes and cook, stirring constantly, for 2 minutes.

Add the stock and bring to a boil; then lower heat and simmer, uncovered, until the noodles are tender. Add parsley, salt and pepper. Serve with crusty French bread.

Serves 4 to 6.

Variation: Add 1/4 cup dry white wine during the last 10 minutes of cooking.

Fijon (Boiled Beans)

1/4 cup olive oil
1 large onion, chopped
1 tablespoon chopped garlic
1 cup tomato paste
1 bunch parsley, chopped fine
7 1/2 cups water
2 cups navy beans
1 teaspoon salt
Pinch dried red pepper, or more to taste

Wash beans and soak overnight.

Heat oil in a heavy pot and sauté the onions until translucent. Stir in garlic and tomato paste. Reduce heat to medium and continue to stir for a minute or two. Add parsley, slowly stir in the water, then add drained beans, salt, and pepper. Cover the pot. Simmer for about 2 hours, stirring occasionally.

Serves 4 to 6.

Fijon (Beef and Bean Stew)

1 pound white navy beans
1/4 cup olive oil
3 large onions, sliced lengthwise to form crescents
1 1/2 pounds stew beef, sliced into thin strips
4 medium tomatoes, cut up
2 tablespoons finely chopped garlic
1 teaspoon paprika
2 teaspoons each salt and pepper
2 1/2 cups beef or chicken stock (approx.)
3 teaspoons dried dill weed
1 bunch parsley, finely chopped (discard stems)

Wash navy beans and soak overnight.

In a large pot, sauté onions in olive oil; add meat and brown. Add tomatoes, garlic, paprika, salt and pepper. Stir well. Drain beans and stir in, adding stock to barely cover; cook on medium heat until liquid is completely absorbed and beans are tender, about 2 1/2 to 3 hours. Add dill and parsley during last 30 minutes. Correct seasoning to taste and serve hot. (Flavor is enhanced if stew is reheated and served the next day.)

Serves 6.

Variation: Substitute lentils for the white navy beans.

Simmered Chick Peas

1 pound dried chick peas
1/4 cup olive oil
1 large onion, coarsely chopped
2 ripe tomatoes, peeled and cut up
Salt and pepper to taste

Soak chick peas overnight in 2 quarts water, or boil for 30 minutes.

Sauté onion in olive oil. Add tomatoes; cook and stir 2 minutes. Drain chick peas and stir into onion mixture. Add water to barely cover and bring to a boil. Lower heat and simmer 1 1/2 hours or until chick peas are tender and liquid is almost completely evaporated. Stir occasionally. Season with salt and pepper. Serve hot or at room temperature.

Serves 6 to 8.

Variation: Substitute lima beans or broad (fava) beans for chick peas.

Beef and Cabbage Stew

3 medium onions, sliced lengthwise to form crescents
1/4 cup olive oil
1 1/2 pounds beef steak, sliced into thin strips
2 tablespoons flour
1 teaspoon each salt and pepper
4 ripe tomatoes, peeled and cut up
1 tablespoon chopped garlic
2 1/2 cups beef or chicken stock
2 small white cabbages, cut in half then sliced into 1-inch wedges
1 bunch parsley, chopped (discard stems)

In a large pot, sauté onions in olive oil until glazed. Add beef and cook until brown. Stir in flour, salt and pepper; cook until the flour absorbs the beef and onion juices. Add tomatoes, garlic, and stock, continuing to cook, and stirring constantly, until sauce thickens slightly. Lower heat and simmer for 30 minutes. Gently stir cabbage into the stew. Add parsley and cook until meat is tender and liquid is reduced by two-thirds.

Serves 6.

Chick Peas in Tomato Sauce

3 tablespoons olive oil
2 medium onions, chopped
3 large cloves garlic, finely chopped
1 green bell pepper, chopped
1 red bell pepper, chopped
3 large ripe tomatoes, chopped
2 tablespoons tomato sauce
1/2 cup finely chopped parsley
Salt and pepper to taste
2 cups cooked or canned chick peas

Sauté onions and garlic in olive oil until tender. Add remaining ingredients (except chick peas), and cook slowly, uncovered, until vegetables are tender and sauce is thickened. Add chick peas and cook for 10 minutes. Serve at room temperature.

Serves 4.

Beef Stew with Potatoes and Cauliflower

1/4 cup olive oil or vegetable oil
4 onions, sliced lengthwise to form crescents
2 pounds lean stewing beef, cut into small pieces
4 cloves garlic, finely chopped
Salt and pepper to taste
3 tablespoons tomato paste
2 to 3 tablespoons red wine vinegar
2 cups beef stock or water
4 or 5 medium potatoes, peeled and quartered
Oil for frying
Fried cauliflower (see recipe)

Heat olive oil in a stew pot and sauté the onions until translucent. Add beef and brown on all sides. Add garlic, salt, pepper, and tomato paste and continue cooking for 1 or 2 minutes. Add vinegar and stock, lower heat to simmer, stir well, and cover. Cook for about 1 1/2 hours until meat is tender.

While the meat is cooking, fry potatoes in a little oil until brown, about 30 minutes, and place in a deep baking dish. Add the cooked meat over the potatoes. Arrange the fried cauliflower florets over the top. Cover and bake in a preheated 425° oven for 30 minutes or until potatoes are tender.

Serves 6.

Fried Cauliflower

1 head cauliflower, broken into florets
3 eggs beaten with 1/2 cup water
2 cups flour
1 teaspoon each salt and pepper
Olive oil for frying

Parboil cauliflower in salted water until just underdone (crisp). Drain. Combine flour with salt and pepper. Dip cauliflower into flour, then egg mixture, then flour. Heat 1/2 inch olive oil in a frying pan and fry cauliflower until golden on all sides. Drain on paper towels, and serve immediately.

Serves 4 to 6.

Garlic Potatoes and Meatballs

1/4 cup olive oil
2 large onions, finely chopped
4 tablespoons tomato paste
2 pounds small new potatoes, peeled
10 cloves garlic, peeled and quartered
1 pound chopped beef
1 clove garlic, finely chopped
Salt and pepper to taste
1 bunch chopped parsley (discard stems)
1 large egg, beaten
1/4 cup bread crumbs
1 teaspoon paprika

In a large pot, sauté half the onions in olive oil until translucent. Add tomato paste and stir in well. Add potatoes, quartered garlic, and water to cover. Bring to boil, then cover and simmer.

While potatoes are cooking, combine the meat, remaining onions, chopped garlic, salt, pepper, parsley (reserving 1 tablespoon for garnish), egg, bread crumbs, and paprika. Shape into balls the size of a small egg. Add to the partially boiled potatoes and continue to cook on low to medium heat until potatoes and meatballs are done. Season sauce with salt and pepper.

To serve, mound the potatoes in the center of a platter and sprinkle with the reserved parsley. Arrange the meatballs around the base of the potatoes and spoon the sauce over the meatballs. Serve hot.

Serves 6.

Euvedge Romanian Stew (Poor Man's Stew)

Meatballs
1 pound lean ground lamb or beef
1/2 cup raw rice
3/4 cup water or tomato juice
3/4 teaspoon each chopped oregano, basil, and dill
1 teaspoon finely chopped garlic

2 tablespoons sesame oil or olive oil
4 medium onions, sliced lengthwise to form crescents
3 tablespoons tomato paste
4 ripe tomatoes
1 cup water
1 medium eggplant, peeled and cut into 1-inch cubes
4 medium zucchini, cut into 1-inch pieces
4 bell peppers (red, yellow or green), cut into strips
1/2 pound green beans, tips removed
Salt and pepper to taste

Combine meatball ingredients and place in refrigerator for 30 minutes to allow rice to absorb the liquid. Shape into small balls.

In a deep, heavy pot, sauté onions in sesame oil until soft. Stir in tomato paste and cook a few minutes. Add tomatoes and water. Stir well. Add meatballs and simmer until they hold their shape, 8 to 10 minutes. Gently fold in remaining vegetables, cover, and cook at medium heat until vegetables are tender and rice is cooked.

Serve 8.

Euvedge with Meat

1 pound stew meat (beef or lamb)
2 onions, sliced lengthwise to form crescents
1/4 cup olive oil
3 ripe tomatoes, peeled and cut up
1 teaspoon finely chopped garlic
1 teaspoon each salt and pepper
1 cup tomato juice
1 eggplant, peeled and cut into chunks
2 long, thin zucchini, sliced thick
1 green bell pepper, sliced thick lengthwise
1/2 pound green beans, ends pinched off and cut in half
3 medium potatoes, peeled and cut into walnut-size pieces

Sauté meat and onions in olive oil until brown. Add tomato, garlic, salt, pepper, and tomato juice and cook on low heat until meat is almost tender. Add remaining vegetables and simmer 30 minutes or until the potatoes are tender. Serve with lots of bread and a green salad.
Serves 6.

Mashed Potato Meatballs

1 large onion, finely chopped
3 tablespoons olive oil or vegetable oil
1 pound cooked ground beef
2 cups cold mashed potatoes
4 large eggs (reserve 1 yolk)
1 bunch chopped parsley (discard stems)
1 teaspoon each salt and pepper
1/3 cup water
Flour
Oil for frying

Sauté chopped onion in olive oil until translucent. Combine with meat, mashed potatoes, 3 eggs, 1 egg white, parsley, salt and pepper. Blend well and shape into meatballs the size of a small egg.
Combine remaining egg yolk with water; dip meatballs in mixture, then roll in flour and flatten. Fry in hot oil on both sides until brown. Place on paper towels to drain. Serve hot with lemon wedges.
Serves 6 to 8.

Lentils with Beef

1 cup lentils
1 pound stew beef, sliced thin, cut into 1″ strips
1/4 cup olive oil
2 medium onions, chopped
1 carrot, sliced thin
2 celery stalks, sliced thin
4 ripe tomatoes, peeled and cut up
2 Turkish laurel or bay leaves
1 teaspoon rosemary
2 to 4 cups tomato juice

Soak lentils in boiling water for 1 hour.

In a stew pot, brown meat in olive oil. Add onions and sauté until translucent. Add carrots and celery and continue to cook. Stir in the tomatoes and herbs; cook for a few minutes and then add lentils and tomato juice to cover. Stir well. Simmer 1 1/2 hours or until juices are almost evaporated and meat is tender. Serve with vinegar on the side.

Serves 6.

Boyos

1-pound loaf stale, dry, crusty bread (French or Italian)
4 large eggs, beaten
1 pound kaseri or Swiss cheese, grated
Salt and pepper to taste
Pinch nutmeg (optional)
2 tablespoons finely chopped parsley
1 large clove garlic, finely chopped
Oil for frying

Break bread into small pieces and soak in cold water until soft, about 5 to 10 minutes. Pick up by the handful and squeeze out all excess water. There should be 3 cups of bread mash. Place in a mixing bowl with the remaining ingredients and mix well.

Drop by tablespoons into hot oil and fry on both sides until golden and firm. Serve hot with soup or salad.

Serves 6.

Variation: Increase the cheese to 1 1/2 pounds, drop by tablespoons onto a greased baking sheet, and bake in a preheated 350°oven for 25 to 30 minutes until golden.

Yogurt Semolina Cake

4 large eggs
1 cup sugar
1 cup yogurt
1/2 cup light vegetable oil (not olive oil)
1 teaspoon each grated orange and lemon zest
Juice of 1 small orange
1 cup coarse semolina farina
1 cup flour
1 teaspoon baking soda

Syrup
2 1/2 cups sugar
2 cups water (or 1 cup orange juice and 1 cup water)

With an electric mixer, beat eggs and sugar until light and fluffy. Mix in yogurt, oil, orange and lemon zest, and orange juice. Combine semolina, flour and baking soda, and add gradually.

Pour into a greased 9 x 13 x 2 baking pan and bake in a preheated 350° oven about 35 to 40 minutes or until top of cake is golden brown. Remove from oven and pour 1 cup hot water over the entire cake and cut into diamond shapes.

Combine syrup ingredients in a small saucepan and boil, stirring until sugar dissolves. Continue to boil for 7 minutes or until liquid becomes sticky.

Pour one-third of the syrup over the cake. Wait until it is absorbed, then add another third. When this is absorbed add the remaining syrup. The cakes will stay fresh for 3 days. Do not refrigerate.

Serves 12 to 14.

Almond Semolina Cake

3 medium eggs
1 cup sugar
1/2 cup water less 2 tablespoons
2 tablespoons vanilla extract
1 cup semolina flour (pasta flour)
1 cup farina
2 cups finely ground almonds

Syrup
1 cup sugar
1 1/2 cups water
Juice of 1 lemon
2 tablespoons rose geranium extract or 1 tablespoon essential oil of rose
    geranium (sold at health food or herb shops)

Make the syrup: Combine sugar, water, and lemon and bring to a boil. Reduce heat and boil gently until the syrup is thickened. Remove from heat and add the geranium extract.

With an electric mixer, beat eggs until light and fluffy. Add sugar, water, and vanilla and mix well. Combine the flours and ground almonds and stir into the egg mixture. Pour batter into a well-greased 8 x 8 x 2 cake pan that has been dusted with flour.

Bake 40 minutes in a preheated 350° oven or until golden and firm. Remove pan from oven and pour 1 cup hot water over the cake. Cut into squares or diamonds and allow to stand in pan for 1 hour, then pour hot syrup over cake. Allow to rest in the pan for about 2 hours.

Serves 12 to 14.

Fried Semolina Squares in Syrup of Vijna

1 egg
2 cups milk
1/2 cup sugar
1 teaspoon vanilla extract
1/2 teaspoon almond extract
1 cup farina

3 egg yolks
1/4 cup water
2 cups crushed butter cookies
Oil for frying
2 cups syrup of vijna (see recipe)

In a blender, mix egg, milk, sugar, vanilla, and almond extract until frothy. Pour into a saucepan and bring to a boil. Lower heat and add farina, stirring constantly until the pudding is a solid mass (spoon should be able to stand up in the pudding). Remove from heat. Spoon into a greased baking pan and smooth out the surface. Refrigerate overnight.

Beat egg yolks with water. Cut pudding into squares; dip in egg yolk, then cookie crumbs. Heat oil and fry until crusty on all sides. Serve with syrup of vijna on the side. May also serve with a dollop of yogurt over each square.

Serves 6 to 8.

Note: Syrup of vijna can be brought at stores selling Middle Eastern food.

Halvah Cake

1/2 cup sesame tahini (sesame paste)
1/2 cup sugar
2 large eggs
1/2 cup flour
1 teaspoon baking soda
1/4 cup water
1 cup semolina flour (pasta flour)
1/4 teaspoon each cinnamon, cardamon, and nutmeg
Orange syrup (see recipe)

Combine the tahini and sugar in a large pot; stir over very low heat until well blended. Remove from heat and add eggs one at a time, mixing well after each addition. Combine flour and baking soda and add, blending well. Add the water and stir until well-blended. Finally stir in the semolina and spices.

Pour batter into a well-greased 8 x 8 x 2 cake pan. Allow to stand for 30 minutes. Bake for 15 minutes in a preheated 400° oven, then 15 minutes at 375°, and 1/2 hour at 350°. Allow cake to cool in the pan.

Cut into squares and pour the hot syrup over the cold cake. Allow to stand in the pan until syrup is almost absorbed. Serve at room temperature.

Serves 16.

Orange Syrup

2 cups sugar
1 cup water
Juice of 1/2 lemon
Juice of 1 orange

Combine ingredients and cook for 20 minutes.

My cousin Jack Sultani in front of his shoe repair shop in Geneva.

Uncle Isaac, Aunt Perla and my cousin Clara in front of their grocery shop. They sold oriental specialties and middle-eastern products.
Geneva, circa 1938.

Grandfather Alchech's shop in Bienne.

My Grandparents' Fruit and Vegetable Cart

Each morning the open air markets sprang up in Geneva's neighborhoods. The aromas of ripe fruit, flowers, pungent cheese, fish and poultry mingled in the air while shoppers purchased their day's supplies from overflowing carts.

My maternal grandparents, Oro and Isaac Benaroya, sold fruits and vegetables at le marché — the open air market — for more than fifty years. Waking long before dawn, they began their day bargaining for cases of produce for all the family members who worked at le marché.

Before World War II, le marché occupied the bridges in Geneva. The merchants sold their produce from wooden carts drawn by horse to the bridges every day. Traffic in those days consisted mainly of pedestrians and bicycle riders. After the war, then the bridges became congested with automobiles, city officials designated other areas of the city for le marché. From then on, my grandparents transported the wooden carts by truck every day and assembled them in the neighborhoods of Coutance, Plain Palais, or Rive, where they exchanged greetings with other vendors as they all busily arranged their wares. The carts were disassembled and trucked away at the end of each day's selling.

At six o'clock in the morning, the customers began arriving. At ten o'clock Grandfather winked at Grandmother and headed for his favorite cafe, where he met his friends for coffee, cards, and backgammon, which he called *Jaquet Turk*. Grandmother liked this arrangement; she preferred to sell alone. On Mondays Grandmother worked a few blocks from home near a fountain that spilled freezing water. I used to watch her amid the crowd, the cart's white canopy fluttering in the breeze overhead, her round face concentrating on her customer's requests. When I appeared, her bright blue eyes met mine and she waved; she loved the conviviality of the market.

Grandmother and Grandfather at le marché.

At home, after work, she rubbed lemon halves over her hands and face to remove the purple fruit stains, and Grandfather, smelling of lavender soap, sat at the dining room table counting the money they earned. Sometimes he allowed a few coins to roll off the table, taking no notice when I scrambled to retrieve them. But a smile spread under his bushy, black mustache.

Everyone begged Grandfather to put his savings in a bank, but he refused. Instead, he kept his gold coins in the dresser drawers, yielding to the family's concern only by locking the bedroom door.

Le marché provided a good living. Family members arriving from Bulgaria and Romania sold produce and new clothes there until they earned enough money to open a shop. Grandmother never wanted to work indoors, but my grandfather, uncles, and aunts opened various shops, which they worked in and owned collectively. A fabric shop sat on the ground floor or my grandparents' apartment house on Rue du Terreaux du Temple, a grocery on Place Longe Mal, and an undergarment shop on Boulevard James Fazy. They also owned an oriental carpet store, a small macaroni factory, and a shoe repair shop.

Grandmother's workday ended at one o'clock. Many afternoons after lunch my grandparents strolled to L'ille Rousseau, a tiny island in the River Rhone. Sometimes they watched the sailboats, at La Potinierre or strolled in the Jardin Englais. Occasionally, they invited their grandchildren to swim at Geneve Plage or the Paqui, a small beach near their apartment.

As evening approached, Grandmother put on a clean white apron and began making decisions about how to use the day's unsold produce. The leaves were removed from old artichokes and the artichoke bottoms used in vegetable stews. Zucchini skins and spinach stems were turned into relish. Nothing was ever wasted. In addition to cooking all kinds of vegetable dishes, Grandmother always started a huge pot of jam. The kitchen shelves held dozens of jam and jelly jars, and these were just the overflow from Grandfather's wine storage closet where she kept most of her preserves.

Grandfather made wine in September and October, when the sweet ripe grapes were harvested. He used methods his forebears learned in Spain. First he washed the grapes and piled them on the kitchen table where he and Grandmother decided which ones to sell at le marché. Then he lugged the grapes he wasn't going to sell to the basement and put them through a hand-cranked wine press. Sometimes Grandfather took the wine press to the vineyard and pressed the grapes there.

Grandfather made sparkling rosé and white wines; he also made peach leaf and plum liqueurs and raki, a strong, syrupy liqueur that was reserved for guests.

It didn't bother Grandfather that it was illegal to make wine at home. He didn't think that he would get caught. Once, though, two men approached his vegetable cart at le marché and asked if they could taste the delicious wine that they had heard he made. Pleased, Grandfather invited them to the house that evening for a tasting.

The strangers drank a few glasses of wine and complimented Grandfather on the bouquet before announcing that they were police. Grandfather had to pay a stiff fine, but he continued making wine as if nothing had happened.

My mother recalled that her introduction to Grandfather's wine took place when she was thirteen. It was an unusually hot evening, and the sound of popping corks could be heard coming from the closet where Grandfather stored his wines. Next, rivers of wine poured from under the closet door. Not wanting to waste anything, the adults in the family started drinking the sparkling wine, trying to finish it before it went flat. Other family members were fetched to join the fun. Mother said she secretly drank six glasses of wine during the turmoil and, feeling very cheerful, stayed up for the impromptu party that lasted until morning.

The following dishes were made with produce from le marché.

Zucchini and Tomatoes

3 ripe tomatoes, cut into wedges
1 medium onion, sliced lengthwise to form crescents
1 teaspoon finely chopped garlic
1/4 cup olive oil or vegetable oil
1 pound zucchini, peeled, sliced 1 inch thick
Salt and pepper to taste
1/4 cup water

Sauté tomatoes, onion, and garlic in olive oil until soft. Add zucchini, salt, pepper, and water. Cover and cook over medium heat until zucchini is tender, about 10 minutes.
Serves 6.

Zucchini Skins I

2 cups loosely packed zucchini skins (4 to 6 medium zucchini)
2 teaspoons olive oil or peanut oil
1 clove garlic, finely chopped
Juice of 1/2 lemon

Peel zucchini with a sharp knife, leaving some of the vegetable attached to the skin; cut into 1-inch pieces. Place all ingredients in a small saucepan and add water to barely cover. Simmer, uncovered, until sauce is reduced and the skins are very tender. Serve at room temperature as a relish.
Serves 4.

Zucchini Skins II

4 to 6 medium zucchini
1/4 cup tomato sauce
2 teaspoons olive oil
Salt and pepper to taste
Juice of 1 lemon, strained

Peel zucchini with a sharp knife, leaving some of the vegetable attached to the skin; cut into 1-inch pieces. You should have about 2 cups skins. Place in a small pan with tomato sauce and olive oil; cover and cook over low heat until tender, about 10 to 15 minutes. Season with salt and pepper, and sprinkle with lemon juice. Serve as an appetizer.
Serves 2 to 4.

Fried Zucchini

4 zucchini, sliced diagonally, 1 inch thick
Salt
2 cups bread crumbs
1 tablespoon finely chopped parsley
3 tablespoons chopped dill weed
1 tablespoon chopped oregano
1 teaspoon pepper
3 eggs, beaten
1/2 cup water
Flour
Oil for frying

Salt zucchini slices and place on several layers of paper towels for 15 minutes; pat dry. Combine bread crumbs with parsley, dill, oregano, and pepper. Combine eggs and water. Dip zucchini in flour, shake off excess, dip in egg mixture, then dip in seasoned bread crumbs.

Fry in hot oil until golden on both sides. Drain on paper towels. Arrange on a serving platter with lemon wedges and sprigs of parsley.

Serves 6.

Variation: Substitute yellow squash or eggplant for the zucchini.

Eggplant Salad I

1 medium eggplant
Salt and pepper to taste
1/2 cup yogurt
2 cloves garlic, crushed

Prick eggplant with a fork and bake on a cookie sheet in a 375° oven for 30 minutes or until the flesh is tender, turning the eggplant several times during baking. Remove from oven and let cool. Cut eggplant in half and scrape the soft flesh away from the skin; place in a bowl (you should have 1 1/2 cups).

Mash or chop the eggplant with salt and pepper until it is smooth. Stir in remaining ingredients. Serve cold with vegetable crudities.

Makes 2 cups. Serves 4.

Note: For a different flavor, cook eggplant on top of gas burner with high flame or under a broiler until skin is charred and flesh tender. Remove skin under cold running water.

Eggplant Salad with Garlic and Cheese

1 medium eggplant
1/4 cup olive oil
Salt and pepper to taste
3 cloves garlic, chopped fine
8 ounces kaseri or Swiss cheese, grated
1 large sweet onion, chopped
3 firm tomatoes, sliced in wedges
Chopped fresh dill or mint

Prick skin of eggplant, place on cookie sheet, and bake in preheated 375° oven for about 30 minutes or until flesh is soft. Cut in half and scrape flesh from skin.

Mash the cooked eggplant until it is smooth. Add oil, salt, pepper, garlic, grated cheese, and chopped onion and stir well. Mound on a platter and surround with the tomatoes. Dust with dill or mint and serve cold or at room temperature.

Serves 4 to 6.

Baked Eggplant

1 medium eggplant
2 medium onions, chopped and sautéed in oil
2 large eggs, beaten
1 cup cottage cheese
1 cup crumbled feta cheese
1 1/4 cups grated kaseri or Swiss cheese
1/2 teaspoon pepper

Prick eggplant with a fork and bake on a cookie sheet in a preheated 375° oven for 30 minutes or until the flesh is soft. Turn the eggplant several times during baking. Remove from oven and let cool. Cut in half and scrape the soft flesh away from the skin and place in a bowl.

Mash eggplant. Add remaining ingredients (reserve 1/4 cup kaseri cheese) and mix well. Pour into a greased baking dish and sprinkle with reserved cheese. Bake in a preheated 350° oven for 45 minutes. Serve hot.

Serves 6.

Variation: Substitute 1 1/2 pounds coarsely grated raw zucchini or chopped spinach for the eggplant. If using spinach, omit the onion.

Eggplant Salad II

1 medium eggplant
5 tablespoons olive oil
3 tablespoons vinegar
1 onion, finely chopped
1 teaspoon each salt and pepper

Prick eggplant with fork and bake on cookie sheet in a 375° oven until the pulp is soft, about 30 minutes. Cut in half and remove the pulp to a bowl and mash or chop until smooth. Add olive oil, vinegar, onion, salt and pepper, and stir. Marinate 1 hour at room temperature before serving. Garnish with black olives, tomato wedges and cucumber slices.
Serves 4.

Variation: Cook eggplant by roasting on top of a gas stove or under a broiler until the skin is charred black. Peel skin off under cold running water. Mash until smooth.

Green Bean Salad

1 pound green beans, tips removed
2 medium onions, sliced lengthwise to form crescents

Dressing
5 tablespoons olive oil
2 tablespoons lemon juice, strained
1 tablespoon vinegar
1/2 teaspoon finely chopped garlic
1/2 teaspoon chopped parsley or mint

Cook green beans in boiling salted water until tender. Drain and place in a bowl; arrange the sliced onions on top. Combine dressing ingredients in a jar and shake well. Pour over the hot beans. Toss the salad and allow to marinate 1 hour. Serve warm or at room temperature.
Serves 4 to 6.

Cooked Spinach Salad

2 pounds fresh spinach
2 tomatoes, cut into wedges
1 cucumber, peeled and sliced
2 carrots, cut into sticks
1 cup cooked or canned chick peas, drained
1 cup canned artichoke hearts, drained

Dressing
1/2 cup olive oil
1/4 cup red wine vinegar
1 teaspoon finely chopped garlic
1/4 teaspoon cumin
1/4 teaspoon cinnamon
Salt and pepper to taste

Remove stems from spinach. Wash spinach several times in cold water until it is free of grit. Cook on low heat for about 5 minutes with only the water that is clinging to the leaves. Stir so that all the leaves are cooked. Squeeze dry.

Arrange spinach in the center of a serving bowl and surround with vegetables. Combine dressing ingredients, pour over all, and let marinate at room temperature for 1 hour.

Serve 4 to 6.

Spinach Stems

3 cups loosely-packed spinach stems, cut into 1-inch pieces
1 tablespoon peanut oil or olive oil
1 garlic clove, finely chopped
Juice of 1/2 lemon

Place all ingredients in a small saucepan and add water to barely cover. Simmer, uncovered, until the stems are tender and almost all liquid has evaporated. Drain remaining liquid and serve in a separate dish. Serve spinach stems as a relish at room temperature or chilled.

Guvetch (Turkish Vegetable Stew)

3 small eggplants, sliced
Salt
Oil for sautéing
2 large onions, sliced
4 slender zucchini, cut into 1-inch pieces
1 pound whole green beans, trimmed
3 ripe tomatoes, chopped
1 pound small young okra, trimmed
3 tomatoes, chopped
2 green bell peppers, sliced
2 red bell peppers, sliced
1/4 cup olive oil
1/2 teaspoon sugar

Salt eggplant slices and place in colander for 30 minutes. Wipe dry and sauté on both sides in oil until just tender.

Place vegetables in a large baking pan in order listed (add eggplant after green beans). Pour olive oil over the top and sprinkle with sugar. Cover pan and bake in a 350° oven until tender, about 1 1/2 hours.

Serves 6.

Variation: Add leftover pot roast or brisket to vegetables during the last 15 minutes of cooking.

Spiced Broccoli

1 bunch broccoli, about 1 1/2 pounds
1/2 cup olive oil or vegetable oil
1/4 cup red wine vinegar
1 teaspoon minced garlic
1/2 teaspoon coarsely ground pepper
1/4 teaspoon each cumin and cinnamon
Salt to taste

Remove the leaves and peel the tough outer part of the broccoli stalks. Cut into florets and slice the stalks in small pieces.

Steam broccoli until bright green and just tender, about 10 minutes. Shake remaining ingredients in a jar and pour over cooked broccoli. Let stand 10 minutes before serving.

Serves 6.

Reyenados (Stuffed Vegetables)

2 small, narrow eggplants, peeled and cut into 3 parts
3 zucchini, cut in half crosswise
6 ripe tomatoes, tops removed (do not discard)
6 bell peppers (green and red), tops and seeds removed
3 medium onions, peeled
2 to 4 tablespoons sesame oil or olive oil
2 cups tomato juice

Stuffing
1 pound lean ground lamb or beef
1/2 cup raw white rice
1 cup water
2 cloves garlic, finely chopped
salt and pepper to taste

Make the stuffing: Combine ingredients and place in refrigerator for 30 minutes to allow rice to absorb the water.

Hollow out centers of vegetables, leaving a shell 1/4 inch thick; save the center portion. Fill shells with stuffing and arrange upright in a baking dish.

Chop onion centers and sauté in sesame oil until translucent. Chop the remaining vegetable centers and add to onions; cook 3 minutes. Add tomato juice and simmer, adding a little water if the sauce becomes too thick. Pour over stuffed vegetables, cover, and bake in preheated 400° oven for 35 minutes or until rice is tender.

Serves 6 to 8.

Turkish Leeks

1 bunch leeks
2 tomatoes, chopped
Juice of 1 lemon
1 tablespoon oil
Salt to taste
1 3/4 cups water

Cut off roots from bulb end of leeks. Remove tough outer leaves and trim off tops. Slice lengthwise and wash thoroughly under cold running water.

Cut into 1-inch pieces and place in a pot with remaining ingredients. Cook uncovered until the leeks are very tender. Serve cold or at room temperature as an appetizer.

Serves 6.

Stuffed Artichokes

4 artichokes
2 cups water
3 tablespoons olive oil

Stuffing
4 cloves garlic, minced
4 tablespoons finely chopped parsley
4 tablespoons finely chopped dill weed
Salt and pepper to taste
1 cup bread crumbs
Juice of 1/2 lemon
2 tablespoons olive oil

Cut stems off artichokes with a knife, and cut 1 inch from leaf tops with a scissors.

Combine stuffing ingredients and push stuffing between the leaves with a spoon. Bring water and olive oil to a boil in a heavy saucepan with a tight-fitting lid. Place artichokes in the pan on a metal steamer; steam for 45 minutes or until artichokes are tender, adding more water if necessary. Serve hot or at room temperature with lemon wedges.

Serves 4.

Fresh Beet Salad

2 bunches small unblemished beets
1 large onion, chopped

Dressing
5 tablespoons olive oil or vegetable oil
Juice of 1 lemon
1 tablespoon vinegar
1 teaspoon each salt and pepper

Scrub beets and trim off tops. Cook, covered, in 1 quart boiling, salted water until tender, about 35 minutes. Peel under cold running water, drain, and slice in rounds.

Combine the dressing ingredients in a jar and shake well. Pour dressing over beets and onions, and toss. Allow to marinate at room temperature for 1 hour before serving.

Serves 4.

Fava Beans and Artichoke Hearts

(My grandmother made this recipe when the artichokes were old and the leaves were no longer usable.)

1 large onion, chopped
2 teaspoons olive oil
2 cup fava beans (about 1 1/2 pound)
1 1/2 pounds artichoke bottoms, cut in chunks
1 or 2 ripe tomatoes, chopped (optional)
1 cup tomato sauce
1 cup finely chopped dill weed
1 cup water
Salt and pepper to taste

Sauté onion in oil until wilted. Add remaining ingredients. Cover and cook slowly until beans are tender. Add more water if sauce becomes too thick.
Serves 6 to 8.

Variation: Use young, spongy, seedless velvety fava pods instead of beans.

Fava Bean Pods

1/4 cup olive oil
1 onion, sliced thickly
2 cloves garlic, minced
1 pound fava beans   (young seedless pods), cut in 1-inch pieces
Juice of 1 lemon

Sauté onions and garlic in olive oil until soft. Add pods and water to cover. Add lemon juice. Cover and cook on low heat until pods are tender.
Serves 6.

Note: Fava bean pods should be soft, spongy and have a very velvety textured surface. When the pods are firm and have a smooth shiny surface, they are mature and the shells are too tough to eat; use only the broad beans inside the shell.

Lemon Okra

1 pound small whole okra
3 tablespoons olive oil
3 large garlic cloves, finely chopped
Juice of 1 lemon
1/3 cup water
Salt and pepper to taste

Cut crowns and stems from okra without exposing the seeds. Place all ingredients in a pan; cover and cook until tender and very little liquid remains. Stir occasionally.
Serves 4.

Fried Okra

Small whole okra
Egg, beaten
Bread crumbs or flour
Vegetable oil

Dip okra in beaten egg, roll in bread crumbs, and sauté in hot oil. Serve with lemon wedges. Serve 3 okra to each person.

Okra and Tomatoes

1 pound small whole okra
3 tablespoons oil (olive, peanut, sesame, or walnut)
2 onions, sliced lengthwise to form crescents
4 ripe tomatoes, chopped
Juice of 1/2 lemon
1/3 cup water
Salt to taste

Cut crowns and stems from okra without exposing the seeds. Sauté onions in oil; add tomatoes and cook until soft. Add okra, lemon juice, water, and salt; cover and simmer until tender.
Serves 6.

Stuffed Green Tomatoes

1 pound ground beef
1/2 cup bread crumbs
1 onion, very finely chopped
1 large egg, beaten
1 cup finely chopped parsley
1 teaspoon each salt and pepper
4 or 5 medium green tomatoes
2 eggs, beaten
1/2 cup flour
Oil for frying

Combine ground beef, bread crumbs, onion, 1 egg, parsley, salt and pepper.

Cut a thin slice off the top of each tomato, scoop out the pulp and discard. Fill tomato shells with meat mixture. Dip each tomato into beaten egg, then in flour. Fry in hot oil on all sides until golden. Place in a baking pan. Bake uncovered in a preheated 325° oven for about 30 minutes or until cooked through.

Serves 4.

Baked Endives with Cheese

2 pounds pale green endive (almost white)
2 tablespoons butter or margarine
2 tablespoon flour
1 cup milk
1/2 teaspoon pepper
1 cup + 3 tablespoons grated kaseri or Swiss cheese

Cut endive into 1-inch pieces; place in boiling salted water and cook for 5 minutes. Drain.

Melt butter, add flour, and cook until flour is light gold in color; slowly add the milk, stirring continuously until mixture is smooth and thick. Stir in pepper and 1 cup cheese. Add endive and stir. Place in a greased baking dish. Sprinkle with remaining cheese and bake in a preheated 350° oven about 25 minutes or until top begins to brown and form a crust.

Serves 6.

Variation: Use chopped, cooked celery stalks or leeks in place of the endive.

Cauliflower and Potatoes with White Sauce

1 head cauliflower
6 medium potatoes, peeled and quartered
2 tablespoons finely chopped parsley

White sauce
3 tablespoons butter or margarine
3 tablespoons flour
1 1/2 cups milk
1/2 pound grated kaseri or Swiss cheese
1/2 teaspoon cumin
Pinch cinnamon

Cut stem off cauliflower and remove leaves; cover with water and cook until tender. In another pan, cook potatoes in salted water. Drain.

While vegetables are cooking, make the white sauce. Melt butter over low heat, add flour, and stir until golden. Add milk gradually and continue stirring until thickened. Add cheese and spices.

To serve, arrange potatoes around whole cauliflower on a platter. Pour sauce over vegetables and sprinkle with chopped parsley.

Serves 6.

Dilled Potatoes and Cauliflower: Omit white sauce. Add 1/2 cup chopped dill weed to 1 stick melted butter or margarine and pour over vegetables.

Mashed Potato Balls

2 cups cold mashed potatoes
4 medium eggs, beaten
4 tablespoons flour
Salt and pepper to taste
3 tablespoons finely chopped parsley
Oil for frying

Combine potatoes, eggs, flour, salt and pepper, and shape into walnut-size balls. Heat oil in a deep fryer and cook a few at a time until puffed and a medium golden color. Drain on paper towels. Serve hot, dusted with parsley.

Makes 2 dozen.

Baked Potato and Cheese Casserole

6 medium potatoes, peeled, sliced into very thin rounds
Salt and pepper to taste
1 to 2 tablespoons very finely chopped garlic
3 cups grated kaseri or Gruyere cheese
1 1/2 cups milk

In a well-buttered casserole, place a layer of potatoes and season with salt and pepper. Sprinkle with 1 teaspoon chopped garlic, then a layer of grated cheese. Add a second layer of potatoes, salt and pepper, garlic, and cheese. Repeat until potatoes and cheese are used up, ending with cheese.

Carefully pour the milk around the edges of the casserole. Bake in a preheated 400° oven for 1 hour or until the cheese on top is brown and crusty and the potatoes are soft.

Serves 6.

Variation: Add 1/4 cup chopped parsley between the layers.

Romanian Pancakes

3 medium potatoes, peeled
1 medium onion, finely chopped
3 tablespoons olive oil
1 pound fresh spinach
3 large eggs, beaten
1/2 teaspoon turmeric
1/2 teaspoon cumin (optional)
1 1/2 teaspoons finely chopped garlic
Salt and pepper to taste
Oil for frying

Boil potatoes until tender; drain and mash. Sauté onion in olive oil until soft and glazed. Wash and dry spinach thoroughly, removing the stems; chop fine. Add to the onions and cook, stirring, for a minute or two. Place in a large bowl and stir in remaining ingredients. If mixture is dry, add another egg.

Heat oil in a large frying pan; add mixture by spoonfuls to form 3-inch pancakes. Fry until golden on both sides. Garnish with tomato wedges.

Serves 6 to 8.

Fried Potatoes

6 medium boiling potatoes, peeled and quartered
Sesame oil or walnut oil
Salt and pepper to taste

Steam potatoes until just underdone. Drain well on paper towels and fry in hot oil until crisp and golden on all sides. Season with salt and pepper.
Serves 4.

Apple Fritters

4 large, firm apples, peeled, cored, and cut into 6 slices each
1 1/2 cups white wine
1/4 cup sugar
1 teaspoon nutmeg
1 teaspoon cinnamon
1 teaspoon vanilla extract
Vegetable oil for frying

Batter
2 cups flour
1 teaspoon baking powder
3 large eggs, beaten
3/4 cup milk
1/2 cup sugar
1 teaspoon vanilla
1/4 teaspoon cinnamon

Combine apples, wine, sugar, and seasonings and macerate for 3 to 4 hours.
Combine batter ingredients. Dip apple slices in batter and fry in vegetable oil until golden on all sides. Serve hot. May roll in sugar or serve with yogurt.

Variation: Fritters can be made with peaches or apricots, cut in half, or peeled pears cut into quarters.

Fruit Tart with Sweet Cookie Dough

1/2 cup unsalted butter or margarine, softened
1/3 cup sugar
1/4 teaspoon salt (optional)
1 large egg plus 1 egg yolk
2 cups flour
8 cups sliced fruit (peaches, apricots, apples, cherries, plums, or prunes)
1 tablespoon flour mixed with 2 tablespoons sugar
3 tablespoons sugar

With an electric mixer, cream butter, 1/3 cup sugar, and salt. Add egg and yolk and mix thoroughly. Add the flour all at once and mix very well. Turn out on a floured work surface and knead 5 minutes. Cut into 2 equal pieces, wrap in wax paper, and allow to rest 1 hour in the refrigerator.

When ready, roll out dough between layers of wax paper and place in two well-greased 12-inch tart pans. Prick dough with a fork for escape of steam. Bake in a preheated 350° oven for 15 minutes. Remove from oven.

Sprinkle bottom of tart shell with flour/sugar mixture. Fill with fruit, arranging fruit slices in neat rings beginning with the outside and working in toward the center. Dust with 3 tablespoons sugar and bake in 350° oven for 20 to 25 minutes. Serve hot, at room temperature, or cold.

Makes two 12-inch tarts. Each tart serves 6 to 8.

Cold Cherry Soup

1 pound red cherries with stems and pits
1 large cinnamon stick
1/2 cup sugar
4 cups water
Juice of one lemon
1 teaspoon kirsch per serving

Place cherries, cinnamon, sugar, and water in a heavy saucepan. Bring to a boil; cover and simmer for 5 to 10 minutes. The cherries should keep their shape. Cool and place in the refrigerator overnight to improve flavor. At serving time, add kirsch to individual goblets. Serve as a dessert or drink.

Serves 4 to 6.

Sweet Tart

1/2 cup butter
1 cup sugar
1 egg plus 1 egg yolk
2 cups flour
1 teaspoon baking powder
2 tablespoons milk
1 teaspoon vanilla
Grated zest of 1 lemon

Filling
Almond Custard (see recipe)
Strawberries, cut in half
Raspberries or blueberries, whole

Cream together butter, sugar, and whole egg. Sift together flour and baking powder; stir half into the creamed mixture. While stirring, add milk and vanilla, then the remaining flour. Mix well and turn out onto a floured work surface and knead 10 minutes. Wrap in wax paper and refrigerate several hours before using.

Roll out dough on floured work surface and place in a well-greased 12-inch tart pan; prick dough with a fork and brush the bottom with beaten egg yolk. Bake 15 to 20 minutes in a preheated 350° oven or until shell is a golden brown. Allow to cool. Fill with almond custard. Carefully arrange fruit in neat rings over the custard, beginning at the outside and working in toward the center. Refrigerate; serve chilled.

Serves 6 to 8.

Almond Custard

1 cup almond syrup (see recipe)
1 cup water or milk
1 envelope unflavored gelatin
1/3 cup cornstarch
2 eggs

Combine all ingredients in a saucepan and mix with a wire whisk (or use a blender). Cook over medium heat until mixture comes to a boil and thickens, stirring constantly. Lower heat and continue stirring 3 to 5 minutes. Pour into serving bowl and refrigerate. Serve with fruit and cookies.
Serves 6.

Note: Almond syrup can be bought at specialty stores selling Middle Eastern foods.

Fruit Soup

2 pounds fresh fruit (combine equal amounts of any of the following: cherries, peaches, apricots, plums, orange or tangerine sections, blueberries, unpeeled nectarines; do not use strawberries or apples)
Juice of 2 lemons
1 cup sugar, or to taste
2 large sticks cinnamon
1 teaspoon kirsch per serving

Remove pits from fruit. Place in heavy saucepan with lemon juice, sugar, and cinnamon sticks; add water to cover. Bring to a boil over medium heat and simmer, covered, for 5 minutes. Let cool, then place in refrigerator overnight. At serving time, add kirsch to individual goblets and stir. Decorate with a fresh mint sprig.
Serves 8.

Variation: Drain fruit, add kirsh, and serve topped with yogurt.

Fruit Tarts with Sweet Yogurt Dough

1/2 cup butter
1/4 cup sugar
1/2 cup yogurt
2 cups plus 1 teaspoon flour
1 egg yolk, beaten
1 tablespoon flour mixed with 2 tablespoons sugar
4 cups fruit (plums, peaches or apples cut in thin wedges; Italian prunes or
    apricots cut in half; pitted whole cherries)
3 tablespoons sugar (approximately)

With an electric mixer, cream butter and sugar. Add yogurt and beat well. Add 2 cups flour all at once and blend thoroughly. Wrap in wax paper and refrigerate 6 hours.

Roll out dough between layers of wax paper until it is at least 14 inches in diameter. Place in freezer for 5 minutes or until firm. Peel off top layer of wax paper and turn over and press dough into a 12-inch tart pan. Peel off remaining wax paper and run a knife along the outer edge of the pan to remove the excess dough hanging over. Brush a thin layer of egg yolk over bottom and sides of crust and stab air holes through bottom surface with a fork.

Bake 15 minutes in a preheated 350° oven. Remove from oven and sprinkle with flour/sugar mixture. Carefully arrange fruit slices in neat rings, beginning at the outside and working in toward the center. Sprinkle with sugar and return to oven; bake about 20 to 25 minutes. Allow to cool to room temperature before serving.

Serves 6 to 8.

Macedonian Fruit Salade

1/2 canteloupe
1/2 Persian melon
3 seedless oranges, in segments
3 large ripe peaches
3 ripe bartlett pears
5 ripe apricots
4 sweet red plums, pitted
1 1/2 cups sweet red cherries, pitted
1/2 cup white raisins
1/3 cup sugar
4 tablespoons Kirsch liqueur

Cut fruit into bite-size wedges and combine in a large salad bowl. Stir in the sugar and liqueur; refrigerate for several hours. Serve cold, garnished with watermelon wedges, pits and rinds removed, fresh whole figs, and pitted dates.

Serves 6 to 8.

Spiced Fruit

2 pounds fruit (pears, plums, peaches, apricots, cherries, or figs)
Butter for sautéing (unsalted)
1/2 cup white vinegar
2 cups sugar
1 tablespoon each whole cloves and whole allspice
1 large stick cinnamon

Remove pits and cut fruit into quarters. Small fruit may be cut in half or left whole. Sauté in a little butter.

Bring remaining ingredients to a boil. Cook gently for 10 minutes. Add the fruit and continue cooking 10 to 15 minutes more, stirring ocasionally; skim surface from time to time. Allow to cool. Refrigerate in a covered container. Macerate 3 days before serving.

Makes one quart.

My brother, my cousin Laurette, Aunt Alice Benaroya and I. On our way to the farm in Versoix, 1953.

Uncle Robert with friends and cousins.

The Sultani, Finzi and Alchech families gathered on a Sunday afternoon.
      La Gabule, France, 1920.

I am at the farm in Versoix.

Mother's sister Mimi with their sister-in-law, Alice. Nyon, 1946.

Uncle Robert and friends at a barn in the middle of his vineyard.

Taking A Tour

Most family members came home for lunch, the main meal of the day. On Switzerland's cold, bright winter days Grandmother often served roast lamb, which she had prepared the night before. As I walked home from school I anticipated the lovely slice of meat covered with gravy.

The most succulent part of the lamb, according to my grandparents, was the head. The head holds seven different kinds of meat. By custom, the oldest and wisest in the family received this prize. When Grandfather popped the lamb's eyes — considered a delicacy — into his mouth and spit out the pips, all the children stopped eating to watch.

Luncheon conversation centered on where to hold the weekly Sunday gathering of family and friends, a ritual we called "taking a tour." The adults entertained the children by debating the advantages and disadvantages of various destinations and by discussing what food to take.

Many times in winter we brought the makings for a thick, hearty soup to the family's farmhouse in the town of Versoix. Once the soup was simmering on the stove, everyone bundled up for tobogganing, skiing, and skating. We returned to the farmhouse whenever we were hungry, to feast on a bowl of delicious soup.

But I preferred going there in the summer when everyone dressed up for a long afternoon of picnicking. The men wore suits, their shirt collars open upon their lapels; the women wore dresses and high heels. My older cousins wore leather pants and hiking boots, and I put on a white dress covered by an apron to keep it clean. Gold earrings dangled from my ears.

At the appointed time, a caravan of cars and bicycles arrived. My uncle brought his truck to take the weary bicycle riders home afterwards. When we got to the farm, everyone helped unpack the food. Then we scattered in all directions to hike, pick wild flowers, or gather the eggplant, okra, artichokes, and fava beans that Grandfather raised for our family meals, since these vegetables weren't readily available in Switzerland at that time. Music from guitars and mandolins drifted into the air and mingled with the cheerful sound of Uncle Mordi playing the spoons.

In the spring, Uncle Robert invited everyone to his chalet, which sat in the center of a vineyard. He traded the vegetables he grew for grapes to make wine. When we arrived for our Sunday visit, we usually found Uncle Robert chasing cows and horses out of his garden. He would come to the car and greet us, complaining about providing lunch for the animals.

After lunch, while the adults relaxed, Uncle Robert took the children to hunt wild mushrooms. He was one of the country's experts on mushrooms. He carefully examined every specimen, checking the books he had brought with him to make sure that the mushrooms were edible. Picking mushrooms, he told us, could be dangerous, but Uncle Robert loved a challenge.

He used to grease his body and swim across the narrow part of the River Rhone in freezing weather or scramble up the mountains to pick edelweiss in the spring. He rode our horses in village races, never winning, but enjoying the fun. He was an ideal uncle.

The places Grandmother chose for Sunday's outings were also my favorites. She like to visit the gypsy camp at La Queue d'Arve. My uncles always brought their mandolins and violins and joined in the lively music. Grandmother encouraged all of us, even the children, to have our palms read.

Grandmother also enjoyed trips into France to Divône or Hermance for gambling. She was lucky at the tables, but Grandfather wasn't. He got grouchy when he lost.

We also used to drive through the countryside and fill baskets with almonds, or we swam in lakes that reflected the surrounding mountains. We went to vineyards where proprietors filled our carafes with wine from huge barrels, or we picnicked at La Gabule on Lake Geneva or at Isle Creux de Chanteaux, where we ate late dinners at wonderful restaurants before going home.

Even in severe weather, the relatives gathered on Sunday. We simply brought food to the synagogue where we played games, listened to music, danced, and discussed the Kabalah and the Bible. It was a very festive time.

These are some of the foods we ate on summer picnics at the farmhouse.

Berenjena Turquese
(Turkish Tomato Eggplant Salad)

3 long, narrow eggplants (about 1 pound each), peeled and thickly sliced
1/2 cup olive oil (approx.)
3 medium onions, sliced lengthwise to form crescents
2 large garlic cloves, finely chopped
5 ripe medium tomatoes, coarsely chopped
1 cup tomato juice
1 tablespoon salt, or to taste
3 tablespoons finely chopped parsley
1 tablespoon red wine vinegar

Sprinkle eggplant slices with salt and place in a colander for 30 minutes. Wipe dry. Cut slices in quarters and sauté lightly in a little olive oil. Remove from pan.

Sauté onions in olive oil. Add garlic and cook for 1 minute. Add tomatoes and cook about 4 or 5 minutes longer. Add tomato juice, eggplant, and salt. Cook over medium heat until eggplant is tender and liquid is reduced, about 30 minutes. Stir in parsley and vinegar. Serve hot or cold.

Serves 6 to 8.

Bell Peppers and Garlic

3 green bell peppers, thinly sliced lengthwise
3 red bell peppers, thinly sliced lengthwise
1/4 cup olive oil
2 teaspoons finely chopped garlic
2/3 cup water
1 teaspoon salt

Sauté peppers in olive oil until wilted. Add garlic, stir, and cook covered for 5 minutes. Bring water and salt to a boil; add peppers, then lower the heat to simmer; stir and cover. Cook until the water is completely evaporated and the peppers are soft and fragrant. Remove to a serving dish and garnish with lemon wedges. Serve at room temperature.
Serves 4 to 6.

Variation: Add 1 tablespoon vinegar just before serving and omit lemons. You may substitute yellow bell peppers.

Pimento Salad

6 bell peppers (red, yellow, and/or green)
1/4 cup olive oil
1/4 cup red wine vinegar
Salt and pepper to taste
1 teaspoon finely chopped garlic
2 tablespoons finely chopped parsley

Char peppers over gas flame or under broiler until black all over. Place in paper bag and close top. Let stand until cool, then wash under cold water and peel off skins. Remove stem and seeds and slice in half. Combine remaining ingredients for dressing; pour over peppers and let marinate several hours at room temperature. Serve with crusty French bread, sliced onions, and black olives.
Serves 4 to 6.

Asparagus and Artichoke Hearts with Dill Sauce

1 pound asparagus, pithy end removed
5 cups water
1 teaspoon salt
2 cups canned artichoke hearts
3/4 cup cooked or canned chick peas

Dill sauce
1 1/2 cups mayonnaise (see recipe)
Juice of 1/2 lemon
3 teaspoons finely chopped dill weed

Drop asparagus into salted boiling water. Cook until tender and bright green. Mound artichoke hearts in center of serving platter. Arrange asparagus, tips out, around the hearts. Combine ingredients for dill sauce and cover hearts with sauce and garnish with chick peas. Refrigerate. Serve chilled.
Serves 4 to 6.

Mayonnaise

2 extra-large egg yolks
1 cup olive oil mixed with 3 cups vegetable oil
3 tablespoons white vinegar mixed with juice of 2 lemons
3/4 teaspoon salt

With an electric mixer, beat egg yolks in the large mixer bowl until lemony in color. Continue beating and add oil slowly, drop by drop at first, then 1 tablespoon at a time, until 1 cup of oil has been used. Slowly add 1 tablespoon vinegar mixture and blend thoroughly.

As you continue to beat, slowly add a very fine stream of oil into the mayonnaise until a second cup has been used. Very slowly add 1 tablespoon vinegar, blending thoroughly to prevent separation. Continue adding oil and vinegar until all has been incorporated into the mayonnaise. Whip in the salt 1/4 teaspoon at a time. Spoon into a dry sterile jar and refrigerate.
Makes 1 quart.

Dressing for Leaf Lettuce Salad

2/3 cup olive oil
1/3 cup red wine vinegar
1 teaspoon finely chopped garlic
3/4 teaspoon each chopped oregano, dill weed, and basil (or 1/4 tsp. dried)
Salt and pepper to taste
1 tablespoon lemon juice (optional)
1 teaspoon Dijon mustard (optional)

Combine all ingredients in a jar and shake well. Makes about 1 cup.

Albondigas Vinaigra (Turkish Sour Meatballs)

1 pound lean ground beef
1 egg, beaten
2 slices white bread, soaked in water and squeezed dry
1 large onion, finely chopped
3 cloves garlic, finely chopped
1/2 cup finely chopped parsley
1/2 teaspoon each cumin, turmeric, and cinnamon
Salt and pepper to taste
Flour
3 eggs, beaten
Olive oil for frying

Sauce
1 large onion, finely chopped
3/4 cup crushed tomatoes and their juice
2 tablespoons sesame oil
1/2 teaspoon sugar
1/2 cup wine vinegar

Gently combine the beef, egg, bread, onion, garlic, parsley, and seasonings and shape into small meatballs or fingers. Roll in flour, beaten egg, and again in flour. Fry in 1/4 inch of olive oil until brown on both sides. Place in baking dish.

Combine sauce ingredients in a saucepan and simmer 10 minutes. Pour over meatballs. Cover and bake for 25 minutes at 350°. Let cool slightly before serving.

Serves 4.

Tomato Salad

6 ripe tomatoes, sliced
2 sweet onions, chopped fine or sliced
2/3 cup olive oil
1/3 cup red wine vinegar
1 teaspoon finely chopped garlic
1 1/2 teaspoons chopped oregano or basil
Salt and pepper to taste

Place tomatoes and onions in serving dish. Mix remaining ingredients and pour over. Marinate at room temperature for 30 minutes.
Serves 4 to 6.

Stuffed Grape Leaves

3 large onions, finely chopped
2 tablespoons olive oil
1 cup raw rice
Juice of 1 lemon
Salt and pepper to taste
2 cups water
1 cup currants (optional)
8-ounce jar grape leaves
Juice of 2 lemons (or more)

Sauté onions in olive oil until light brown. Add rice, lemon juice, salt, pepper, and water. Cover and cook on low heat until the rice is tender. Stir in currants.

Rinse grape leaves in cold water; drain. Spread leaves on paper towels. Remove stems and open flat, rib-side up.

To fill the grape leaf, place a heaping teaspoon of rice mixture near the stem end and fold the stem end over the rice; fold the two sides over the rice; tightly fold or roll toward the pointed tip of the leaf, sealing in the rice as if in an envelope.

Place close together in a large pan, fold side down. Add lemon juice and water to cover. Simmer, partly covered, for 1 hour or until grape leaves are tender. Serve hot, room temperature, or cold.
Serves 6.

Tarama

2-1 pound loaves stale, dry, French or Italian bread, crust removed
10-ounce jar carp roe caviar
3 large cloves garlic, crushed in a garlic press
Juice of 3 lemons
4 cups olive oil

Cut bread into large chunks. Add cold water and soak for 10 minutes. Drain in a colander, then squeeze out all the water with your hands (there should be 4 cups, firmly packed).

With an electric mixer, whip the caviar until smooth. Add bread a little at a time, beating until the mixture is creamy. Add garlic and lemon juice and beat 5 minutes longer. With mixer at high speed, add oil very slowly. The mixture should be pale in color and smooth like heavy mayonnaise. Refrigerate.

Serve with sliced tomatoes, cucumbers, black olives, sliced onions, and black bread.

Makes 8 cups.

Parsley Meatballs

2 pounds lean ground meat
5 cups finely chopped parsley
4 large eggs, slightly beaten
1 cup bread crumbs
2 teaspoons finely chopped garlic
1 teaspoon paprika
1 tablespoon chopped dill weed
1 teaspoon each salt and pepper
1 teaspoon cumin
1 egg yolk beaten with 1/3 cup water
Flour
Oil for frying

Combine meat, parsley, eggs, bread crumbs, and seasonings. Mix well, and shape into ovals. Dip into egg-water mixture. Roll in flour and shape into fingers. Fry on all sides until done. Serve with lemon wedges or red wine vinegar.

Serves 8 to 10.

Variation: Stuff finger rolls with seasoned cooked rice before dipping in egg and flour.

Almond Chicken

6 drumsticks, skins removed
6 thighs, skins removed
3 breasts, skinned, boned, and split
Flour
4 eggs, beaten
3 cups almond meal (grind about 12 oz. blanched almonds in blender
   or food processor)
Olive oil or vegetable oil for sautéing

Roll dry chicken in flour, then in beaten egg, and last in almond meal. Sauté in oil until golden. Bake in a preheated 350° oven for 25 minutes. Serve hot or cold with lemon wedges.
Serves 6 to 8.

Keftes

1 pound ground lamb or beef
2 eggs, beaten
1 large bunch parsley, finely chopped (stems removed)
1/2 teaspoon cumin
1 teaspoon finely chopped garlic
1 tablespoon finely chopped dill weed
Salt and pepper to taste
Flour
Olive or vegetable oil for frying

Stuffing
1 cup cooked rice
1/4 cup sesame seeds or poppy seeds
Salt and pepper to taste
1 onion, finely chopped

Combine lamb, eggs, parsley, cumin, garlic, dill, salt and pepper. In another bowl, combine stuffing ingredients. Make meatballs the size of a small egg, and push your finger into the center to form a hollow for the stuffing. Press about 2 teaspoons of stuffing in the opening and close tight at both ends. Shape into finger rolls, lightly roll in flour and fry in 1/4 inch oil until brown on both sides. Add more oil to pan when necessary. Serve with lemon wedges.
Serves 4.

Keftes de Prassa (Leek Meatballs)

1 bunch leeks
1 1/2 cups salted water
2 pounds lean ground beef
4 eggs, beaten
1 teaspoon each cumin, tumeric, salt, and pepper
2 teaspoons finely chopped garlic
1/4 cup dill weed (or 2 teaspoons dried)
1/4 cup sesame seeds
Flour
Olive or vegetable oil for frying

Cut off roots from bulb end of leeks. Remove tough outer leaves and trim off tops. Slice lengthwise and wash thoroughly under running water. Slice into 1/2-inch pieces. Bring salted water to a boil, add leeks, and simmer 10 minutes or until leeks are tender. Drain in a colander and squeeze all water from leeks.

Combine remaining ingredients (except flour and oil), add leeks, and blend gently. Shape into meatballs and roll in flour. Flatten meatballs a little and fry in 1/4 inch oil until brown on both sides. Add more oil to pan when necessary. Serve with lemon wedges or red wine vinegar.

Serves 6 to 8.

Variations: You can substitute 5 cups finely chopped parsley or scallions for the leeks. The beef mixture can be shaped into finger rolls, stuffed with cooked rice, and fried in olive or sesame oil. Or you can barbecue the meatballs after coating them with flour.

Spiced Veal Tongue

2-pound fresh veal tongue
2 onions, sliced lengthwise to form crescents
1/4 cup olive oil
2 1/2 cups water
2 whole cloves
1 teaspoon chopped garlic
2 Turkish laurel or bay leaves
1 1/2 teaspoons chopped rosemary
1 1/2 teaspoons chopped thyme

In a heavy pot, sauté the tongue and onions in olive oil until tongue is lightly brown all over and onions are translucent. Add remaining ingredients. Cover and simmer 1 1/2 hours or until tongue is tender (test with fork after one hour). Remove from liquid. Slice and serve hot or cold with its own piquant sauce.
Serves 12.

Steak in Wine Sauce

2 onions, chopped
1 teaspoon finely chopped garlic
1/4 cup olive oil
1/2 pound flank steak, sliced very thin
2 tablespoons finely chopped dill weed
Salt and pepper to taste
3/4 cup crushed ripe tomatoes
2 tablespoons vinegar
1/4 cup red wine

Sauté onions and garlic in oil until soft. Cut steak into 1-inch strips; add to onions and sauté until meat loses its red color. Add remaining ingredients and cook uncovered until sauce is reduced by half. Serve with rice.
Serves 4.

Stuffed Grape Leaves in Tomato Sauce

1 pound ground beef or lamb
3 large onions, finely chopped
1 cup raw rice
1 cup water
1 tablespoon garlic
1/4 cup finely chopped dill weed
1/4 cup finely chopped parsley
1 teaspoon salt
1/2 teaspoon pepper (optional)
12-ounce jar grape leaves
1/4 cup olive oil
6-ounce can tomato paste
2 1/2 cups water
Juice of 2 lemons
1 tablespoon vinegar

Combine ground meat, onions, rice, water, garlic, dill, parsley, salt and pepper. Blend thoroughly and set aside.

Heat olive oil and tomato paste in a heavy pot; stir and cook for 2 minutes. Add water, lemon juice, and vinegar and cook together for a few minutes; pour into a bowl.

Rinse grape leaves in cold water; drain. Spread leaves on paper towels. Remove stems and open flat, rib side up. To fill the grape leaf, place a heaping teaspoon of meat mixture near the stem end and fold the stem end over the meat; fold the two sides over the meat; tightly fold or roll toward the pointed tip of the leaf, sealing in the meat as if in an envelope.

Pour a little sauce into the pot. Arrange a layer of stuffed grape leaves close together in the pot, fold side down. Add some sauce, then another layer of grape leaves. Continue with remaining grape leaves. (If there is any meat mixture left in the bowl, make small meatballs and add to the pot.) Pour remaining sauce over all. Cover and simmer about 1 hour or until the rice is tender.

Makes 2 to 3 dozen.

Gourambiedes (Almond Butter Cookies)

1 pound unsalted butter
1 egg yolk
1/2 cup confectioners' sugar
1/2 teaspoon almond extract
1/4 cup water
1 ounce ouzo, a Greek liqueur
3 cups unbleached flour
1 cup rice flour
1/2 cup almond meal or walnut meal
Confectioners' sugar

With an electric mixer on high speed, whip butter until soft and white. Add egg yolk, sugar, almond extract mixed with water, and raki. Beat until smooth and thick, about 5 minutes.

Sift flours together. Measure 4 cups and add to butter mixture; mix well. Turn out onto floured work surface and knead about 5 minutes, adding almond meal while kneading. Divide dough into three pieces; wrap in wax paper and refrigerate for 2 hours.

Pinch off pieces of dough the size of a walnut and roll into 2-inch ropes. Shape into crescents and place on ungreased cookie sheet. Do not crowd. Bake 20 to 25 minutes in a preheated 350° oven. Remove from cookie sheet to a rack. Sprinkle with sifted confectioners' sugar while still hot. Let cool several hours.

Makes about 3 dozen.

Almond Crisps

3 cups almond meal (grind about 12 oz. blanched almonds in blender
   or food processor)
4 tablespoons rice flour
4 egg whites, room temperature
Pinch cream of tartar
1 1/4 cups confectioners' sugar, sifted

Sift almond meal and flour together and set aside. Whip egg whites with cream of tartar until stiff. Gradually add sugar and continue to whip. Fold in flour mixture. Drop batter by spoonfuls on a greased cookie sheet and bake in preheated 300° oven for 45 minutes.

Makes about 2 dozen.

Sesame Biscotchos

These cookies were served with a drink of syrup of vijna mixed with water or an almond cooler to break the fast at the end of Yom Kippur.

3 large eggs
1 cup sugar
1/2 cup oil
1 teaspoon baking powder
Grated zest and juice of 1 orange
4 1/2 cups flour
1 egg yolk, beaten
Sesame seeds

With an electric mixer, cream eggs, sugar, and oil. Add baking powder and mix well. Add orange zest and juice and beat mixture together thoroughly. Add flour 1/2 cup at a time. When flour is totally incorporated, turn dough out onto a lightly floured surface; dough should be supple and easy to roll out. Roll out to 1/4-inch thickness with a floured rolling pin; slice into squares. Brush top with the egg yolk and press wet surface into sesame seeds. Place cookies on a well-oiled baking pan and bake 20 minutes in a preheated 350° oven.

Makes 2 dozen.

Fresh Sour Cherry Cake

2/3 cup butter
2/3 cup sugar
1 teaspoon grated lemon zest
6 extra-large eggs, separated
1/3 cup milk
1 1/3 cups flour
1 teaspoon baking soda
1 1/2 pounds fresh sour cherries, pitted
Confectioners' sugar

With an electric mixer, beat egg whites until stiffs, set aside. Cream butter, sugar, lemon zest, and egg yolks. Stir in milk. Sift flour and baking soda together and add. Gently fold in the egg whites until completely combined. Pour into a greased and floured 9 x 13 cake pan and cover with cherries.

Bake in a 350° oven for 45 minutes to 1 hour or until done. (The cherries will sink into the cake). Cool and dust with confectioners' sugar.

Variation: Grease and flour the cake pan. Sprinkle with 1/4 cup sugar. Arrange the cherries in tight circles, and sprinkle with another 1/4 cup sugar. Pour batter into the pan and bake as above. When done, pour hot Baklava syrup (see recipe) over the cake. Allow to cool to room temperature before removing from pan.

Father and a fellow soldier in the Turkish army, 1929.

Father with his parents, Mathilde Finzi-Alchech and Leon Alchech.

Wedding portrait of Mathilde and Leon Alchech, 1900.

My great-grandfather, Rabbi Alchech Marseille, circa 1880.

Making Multilayered Treats

My grandmother, the second youngest of twelve children, was born in Romania of Sephardic parents who had previously lived in Turkey for many years. When the family moved to Greece, neighbors taught Grandmother to speak Greek and to make appetizers and desserts with a flaky pastry called filo.

When Grandmother lived in Greece she could buy the freshly-made filo pastry at the neighborhood bakeries, but when she came to Geneva she had to make her own dough. My mother and aunts helped with the arduous task, knowing that they would be rewarded with portions of the pastry. Making the dough, which was just flour, water and oil, was easy, but manipulating it into the delicate paper-thin sheets was very tricky.

Grandmother's procedure was to place the lump of dough on a table covered by a white tablecloth. Simultaneously, my mother and aunts put their oiled hands, palms down, underneath the dough and began stretching it with their fingertips until it covered the table top. They worked fast because if the dough dried, it cracked.

When the dough finally hung over the table's edge, they lifted the cloth and, holding it taut, carried it to Grandmother's bed where they continued to stretch it until the dough was transparent and grazed the floor. At this point Grandmother cut the pastry into large pieces with a scissors and wrapped the pieces in a damp towel until she needed them.

Even then, I understood that there was more to these communal cooking sessions than just the delicious treats. Cooking together provided companionship and time to laugh and talk without interruption. I recall my aunts and grandmother exchanging gossip. When they touched on a particularly spicy subject, they would switch from speaking

French to Judizmo so that children wandering into the kitchen wouldn't understand.

The following recipes may be made with commercially made filo, defrosted overnight in the refrigerator.

Borekitas Espinaca (Spinach Turnovers)

1 pound filo (24 sheets)
1 cup corn oil or peanut oil
1/2 pound butter or margarine, melted

Filling
1 pound pot style cottage cheese or farmers cheese
1/2 pound Swiss cheese, shredded
1/4 pound feta cheese, finely crumbled
3 medium potatoes, boiled and mashed smooth
6 medium eggs
1 teaspoon finely chopped garlic
1 pound fresh spinach, finely chopped
Salt and pepper to taste

Combine filling ingredients and mix well. Unroll filo and cut in half lengthwise. Combine oil and butter. Take one sheet and brush with oil mixture. Fold in half lengthwise and brush the top with oil mixture. Place a heaping teaspoon of filling at the short end of the strip. Fold in the sides 1/2 inch. Begin folding into triangles, as if folding a flag. End with a neat triangle. Brush both sides of pastry with oil mixture. Place on greased baking sheet.

Continue same procedure with the remaining filo dough. Bake in a preheated 350° oven about 35 to 40 minutes or until golden brown.

Makes about 4 dozen.

Note: Can be frozen. Bake frozen in preheated 350° oven for 50 minutes.

Pastel Berenjena (Eggplant Pie)

1 pound filo (24 sheets)
1 cup corn oil or peanut oil
1 cup butter or margarine, melted

Filling
1 large eggplant
1 pound pot style cottage cheese or farmers cheese
1/2 pound Swiss cheese, shredded
1/4 pound feta cheese, finely crumbled
3 medium potatoes, boiled and mashed smooth
6 large eggs
1 teaspoon garlic, chopped fine
3 medium onions, chopped and sautéed until translucent
Salt and pepper to taste

Prick eggplant with a fork and place on a cookie sheet. Bake at 375° for 20 to 30 minutes or until flesh is tender, turning eggplant several times during baking. Cut in half and scrape flesh from skin. Mash or chop flesh.

Combine eggplant with remaining filling ingredients. Combine oil and butter. Brush a 9 x 14 baking dish with the oil mixture. Put a sheet of filo in the dish and brush with oil mixture. Repeat until you have 8 sheets. Place a layer of filling over the top sheet. Add 8 more sheets, brushing each sheet with oil mixture. Add a layer of filling and 8 more oiled sheets. Brush top with oil mixture and freeze for 30 minutes. Using a very sharp knife cut across the length of pie, then cut diagonally in strips 2 inches wide, to make a diamond design.

Bake in a preheated 400° oven for 20 minutes, turn oven down to 350° for 30 minutes, then turn to 300° for 30 minutes. Let cool in pan and recut diamonds.

Serves about 20.

Bulemas (Cheese Filled Coils)

1 pound filo dough (24 sheets)
1 cup corn oil or peanut oil
1 cup butter or margarine, melted

Filling
1 pound pot style cottage cheese or farmers cheese
1/2 pound kaseri or Swiss cheese, shredded
1/4 pound feta cheese, finely crumbled
3 medium potatoes, boiled and mashed smooth
6 large eggs
1 teaspoon finely chopped garlic
Salt and pepper to taste

Combine the filling ingredients and mix well. In a separate bowl, combine oil and butter; brush onto surface of one sheet of filo, fold in half lengthwise, and brush over top. Spoon a thin line of filling along the longest open edge. Fold both short sides in 1 inch. Starting with the filling end, roll into a long, tight rope. Brush seam with oil mixture and, keeping seam on the inside, gently roll into a coil, taking care not to break. Place coil in a greased baking pan and brush top of coil with oil mixture.

Repeat with remaining 23 sheets of dough, leaving about 1 inch between coils. Bake in a preheated oven at 350° for 35 to 40 minutes or until golden brown.

Makes 2 dozen.

Note: May be frozen unbaked. Bake frozen in preheated 350° oven for 50 to 55 minutes.

Nut Rolls

1 pound filo dough (24 sheets)
1 pound butter or margarine, melted

Filling
1 cup ground walnuts
1 cup ground almonds
1/2 cup sesame seeds
1/4 cup poppy seeds
2 cups sugar
1 teaspoon cinnamon
1/2 teaspoon cardamon

Combine filling ingredients. Brush melted butter on surface of 1 sheet of filo and fold in half lengthwise. Brush new surface with butter, turn over and brush other side. Spoon a line of nut mixture across the short end. Fold in sides so that they meet in the center and roll into a cigar shape. Grease edge to seal. Repeat until filling is used up. Place on greased baking pan, seam side down. Grease top. Bake in preheated 350° oven for 35 minutes. Dust with mixture of sugar and cinnamon and return to oven for 5 minutes. Let cool on serving platter. Serve at room temperature.

Makes about 24.

Variation: Serve with syrup (recipe, see Baklava) in place of sugar and cinnamon, omitting final 5 minute baking.

Baklava

1 pound unsalted butter or margarine
1 1/2 cups light vegetable oil
48 sheets filo dough (about 2 pounds), fresh or frozen.
   If frozen, defrost in refrigerator for 1 to 2 days
   and bring to room temperature before opening package.

Syrup
3 cups sugar
1 1/2 cups water
Juice of 2 to 3 oranges
Juice of 1 lemon
3/4 teaspoon cinnamon
3/4 teaspoon cardamon (optional)

Make syrup: Bring sugar, water, orange juice, and lemon juice to a boil in a deep saucepan. Cook over low to medium heat until the syrup is thickened and clear, about 30 minutes. Remove from heat and stir in the spices. Refrigerate for 12 to 24 hours for best results.

Melt butter and oil in a saucepan. Combine ingredients for selected filling. Use a pastry brush to generously grease the bottom and sides of a 10x14x2 baking pan (the pan may be larger so long as it is no larger than the filo sheets; you may have to fold ends of sheets to fit the pan).

Place 12 sheets of filo in the bottom of the pan, brushing some butter/oil over each layer. Spread with one-third of the filling. Repeat (12 sheets filo, butter/oil, one-third filling). Repeat again, ending with a layer of 12 sheets filo and butter/oil. Cut the last sheet of filo dough to fit the pan and brush the top with the butter/oil mixture. Place pan in freezer for 30 minutes.

Using a very sharp knife, cut the baklava lengthwise into 5 or 6 rows of equal width. Then cut diagonally through the rows to form the traditional diamond shapes.

Preheat the oven to 400°. Bake 15 minutes at 400°, 15 minutes at 350°, and 1 hour at 300°. Pour cold syrup over the hot baklavah. Allow to cool to room temperature and recut the diamonds. Remove to individual fluted paper cups.

Makes approximately 36 diamond-shaped pieces. (The triangles are saved for the children.)

Filling 1
1 pound ground walnuts or almonds (or combination)
1 tablespoon cinnamon
2/3 cup sugar

Filling 2
2 pounds ground unsalted pistachio nuts
1 tablespoon cinnamon
1 1/4 cup sugar
(1 1/2 teaspoon rosewater added to cold syrup)

Filling 3
1 cup ground almonds
1 cup ground walnuts
1 cup ground hazelnuts
1/2 cup poppy seeds
1/2 cup sesame seeds (hulled)
2 teaspoons cinnamon
1/4 teaspoon cardamon
2/3 cup sugar
(1 tablespoon orange blossom water added cold to syrup)

Kadayif

1 pound kadayif dough (sold frozen in shops selling Greek food)
1 pound unsalted butter or margarine, melted
1 cup corn oil or peanut oil
Syrup (recipe, see Baklava)

Filling
3 cups ground walnuts or almonds (or a combination)
3 teaspoons cinnamon
2/3 cup sugar

Grease a 10 x 14 x 2 baking pan. Gently pull apart the shredded dough in a large bowl; combine melted butter and oil and pour over dough. Continue unrolling the dough until it is completely open and covered with the butter mixture.

Combine filling ingredients. Divide dough into thirds. Spread out one-third of the dough in the pan, and cover evenly with half the filling. Repeat layers, ending with the dough.

Place in freezer for 30 minutes so that it will be easy to cut in diamonds (see Baklava recipe for instructions). Preheat oven, bake 15 minutes at 400°, 15 minutes at 350°, and 1 hour at 300°. Pour cold syrup over hot kadayif. Cool to room temperature and recut diamonds. Serve in individual fluted paper cups.

Serves 25.

Tish Pishti I

Tish Pishti was always served on Rosh Hashana.

Syrup
2 cups sugar
1 cup water
Juice of 2 oranges
1 tablespoon grated orange zest
Squeeze of lemon juice

Combine ingredients in a saucepan and bring to a boil. Cook over low to medium heat until syrup is thickened and clear.

Filling
1 pound coarsely ground walnuts or almonds
1 tablespoon cinnamon
2/3 cup sugar
1 teaspoon grated orange zest

Combine ingredients.

Dough
1 cup water
1 cup oil
1/2 cup sugar
2 cups flour
12 to 16 perfect walnut halves or whole almonds (same nut as in filling)

In a large saucepan, bring water, oil, and sugar to a boil. Reduce heat to simmer and slowly add flour, stirring with a wooden spoon until the dough pulls away from the sides of the pan. Remove from heat and divide into two equal parts. Spread half the dough in a greased 8 x 8 x 2 baking pan. Cover with the filling, then with the remaining dough. Cut into diamond shapes (see Baklava recipe for instructions). Place a nut in the center of each diamond.

Bake in a preheated 350° oven for 50 to 60 minutes or until golden brown. Recut the diamonds and pour the cool syrup over while hot. Allow to stand at room temperature until cake is cold and all the syrup is absorbed. Serve at room temperature. Will keep for several days.
Serves 12.

Tish Pishti II

Syrup
1 cup sugar
1 cup water
Juice of 2 oranges
Juice of 1 lemon
1 cinnamon stick

Combine all ingredients except the cinnamon, and bring to a boil. Reduce heat and simmer for 10 to 15 minutes; remove from heat and add the cinnamon. Allow to rest until the following day. Remove the cinnamon before pouring over the cake.

Filling
6 ounces ground walnuts
2 teaspoons cinnamon
1/4 teaspoon cloves
Grated zest of 1/2 orange
1/2 cup sugar

Combine all ingredients.

Dough
2/3 cup vegetable oil or olive oil
1/3 cup olive oil
1/2 cup water
2 tablespoons sugar
3 to 4 cups flour
16 perfect walnut halves

In a saucepan, combine oils, water, and sugar and bring just to boiling point, but do not boil. Remove from heat and let cool until you can put your finger in the liquid for 4 seconds. Mix in the flour by 1/2 cupfuls until the dough pulls away from the sides of the pot; discard leftover flour.

Lightly oil an 8 x 8 x 2 baking pan. Divide dough into 2 equal parts and place one-half in the pan, spreading out to cover the entire bottom. Cover evenly with filling and then with remaining dough. Gently press the walnut halves on top of cake, evenly spaced.

Bake in a preheated 350° oven for 50 minutes. Remove from oven and cut into squares. Slowly pour cold syrup over the hot cake and let rest until the cake is cold and the syrup has been absorbed.

Makes 20 pieces.

Grandmother and Grandfather with my mother, her sister Mimi, and brothers David and Robert.

Isaac and Perla Pinhas

Isaac and Oro Benaroya.
Geneva, 1915.

Grandfather Isaac Benaroya,
waiting for the train to
Hermance, 1938.

Sabbath

The Sabbath, Saturday's day of rest, began at sundown on Friday with a short service at the synagogue. Then the family gathered at Grandmother's for dinner. The meal was a celebration of the arrival of the Sabbath Queen, an endearing name given to the Sabbath because of its special place in Jewish life. It is the most important of Jewish holidays.

My cousins and I helped prepare the meal by slicing vegetables, shelling almonds, and washing the pots and pans used by the busy cooks. These tasks were part of the apprenticeships served by the grandchildren until they were old enough to cook. Sometimes eight of us worked in the kitchen at once, but everyone knew what to do and things ran smoothly.

Whenever I visited our basement storeroom to fetch potatoes, Grandfather followed with the key and lantern because he knew that the dark, musty place scared me. I called it *"la cave."* The storeroom also held old paintings, antiques and, at the far corner, the wine press. The lantern lit only a small part of the room. I was always glad to get back upstairs where a fire warmed the dining room and fresh flowers sweetened the air. I set the table with Grandmother's stiff, white tablecloth and her fine china and silver; then I placed a white napkin over the two loaves of challah.

When all was ready, Grandmother lit the oil lamps, each filled with the proper amount of oil to insure burning throughout the Sabbath. Grandfather's homemade wine released everyone's good spirits. We usually had guests for dinner because it was a tradition that if we discovered strangers attending services at the synagogue, we invited them home for the Sabbath meal.

The next day my parents, aunts, and uncles let the peaceful mood of the day take over. They left their business worries behind as they enjoyed a steady stream of visitors. Each new arrival participated in a centuries-old Sephardic tradition to honor guests: a spoonful of homemade jam shimmering in a crystal bowl, a small glass of water to cleanse the sweetness, a demitasse of thick, rich Turkish coffee followed by another glass of water, and finally, delicious confections served from silver trays. A samovar of tea and a pitcher of cream sat at one end of the table.

Meanwhile the children, giggling and consuming large quantities of wonderful sweets, whisked away the half-empty trays and replenished them in the kitchen.

The Sabbath meal, the most elaborate of the week, began with a light soup followed by a fish course. Since everything was prepared ahead of time, there was no last-minute cooking. We ate fresh fruit for dessert, saving the sweets for Saturday's visitors.

Avgolomeno (Lemon Chicken Soup)

1 soup chicken, cut into serving pieces
1/4 cup olive oil
Salt and pepper to taste
1/4 cup flour
2 eggs, beaten
Juice of 1 lemon, strained

Sauté chicken in olive oil. Season with salt and pepper. Add water to cover and bring to boil, skimming the surface from time to time during the cooking. Cover pot and simmer until chicken is tender. Remove cooked chicken, bring the stock to a boil, and cook 15 minutes to reduce the volume.

Remove about 1/2 cup of the stock and slowly blend it into the flour, 1 tablespoon at a time. In another bowl add the lemon juice to the eggs. In a large sauce pan, combine the egg mixture with the flour mixture. Cook gently, stirring with a wooden spoon, until it begins to thicken and is creamy. Continue adding chicken stock by tablespoons, stirring constantly, until you have used one-fourth of the stock, then gradually increase the quantity and rate of adding the stock. When half the liquid has been stirred in, pour mixture back into the soup pot. Stir well.

Bone and slice the chicken; return to the soup. Adjust seasonings. Sprinkle with chopped dill or parsley and serve hot.

Serves 4 to 6.

Variation: You may add 1 1/2 cups cooked white rice to the soup just before serving.

Sabbath Challah

Sponge
4 cups unbleached white flour
3 packages dry yeast
1 tablespoon sugar
1 cup tepid water (about 101° F)

3 large eggs, room temperature
1/3 cup sugar (heaping)
1/2 cup peanut oil
1 tablespoon salt
1 cup tepid water
3 to 4 cups flour
1 egg, beaten
Poppy seeds

For the sponge, place flour in a large bowl. Make a well in the center and add yeast, sugar, and water. With a fork, mix the ingredients in the well, combining with some of the surrounding flour, until mixture is the consistency of thin pancake batter. Cover bowl and let stand for 20 minutes.

Add 3 eggs, sugar, oil, and salt and mix well. Add water, 1/2 cup at a time, mixing well after each addition. Add 3 cups flour, one at a time, mixing well. The dough may be somewhat sticky.

Turn out onto work surface that has been spread with flour. Dust entire surface of dough with flour and gather it together. Knead gently but firmly for 5 minutes, adding a little flour to keep dough from sticking to the hands.

Place dough in large greased bowl, cover with a towel, and place in a warm draft-free place. Let rise until double, about 1 1/2 hours. Punch down and let rise again for about 1 hour. Turn out onto lightly-floured work surface and divide in half. Cover one piece and set aside.

Cut other piece into 3 equal parts. Roll each part into a "rope" about 15 inches long and 1 1/2 inches thick. Braid ropes together and moisten ends with a little water to seal. Place on lightly-greased baking sheet. Repeat procedure with reserved dough. Let loaves rise for 30 minutes. Brush with the beaten egg and sprinkle with poppy seeds.

Bake each loaf separately in a preheated 375° oven for about 25 minutes or until loaf sounds hollow when tapped. Let cool on wire rack.

Makes 2 loaves.

Carp Fillets in Tomatoes and Parsley

2 pounds carp fillets (or any light fish fillets such as flounder, sole, turbot)
1 large onion, finely chopped
1 large bunch parsley, chopped (discard stems)
1/4 cup olive oil
1 teaspoon very finely chopped garlic
4 medium tomatoes, peeled and cut in wedges
Juice of lemon
1/2 cup water
Salt and pepper to taste

Sauté onions and parsley in olive oil until onions are translucent. Stir in garlic and tomatoes and cook a few minutes. Add lemon juice, water, salt, and pepper and stir well. Add the fish and simmer for 10 to 15 minutes until it become opaque. Serve hot or at room temperature.

Serves 4.

Deep Fried Fish

1 pound boneless fillet of fish, sliced in 1-inch strips
1 cup milk
1 cup flour
4 egg whites
1/2 cup olive oil
1/2 teaspoon each salt and pepper, or to taste
1/2 cup warm water
1 package dry yeast
Oil for frying
Chopped parsley

Soak fish in milk for several hours (or overnight in the refrigerator if the fish is frozen).

Combine flour, egg whites, olive oil, salt, pepper, water, and yeast; mix into a smooth paste, the consistency of very heavy cream. Allow to rest 2 hours in a warm, draft-free place.

Drain fish and rinse; dry on paper towels. Heat oil. Dip fish fillets in the batter and drop into the hot oil; fry until golden. Sprinkle with chopped parsley and serve immediately with lemon wedges.

Serves 3 to 4.

It was our custom to serve this with salad and roasted potatoes.

Fish in Wine Sauce

1 1/2 pounds fish fillets
Flour
Salt and pepper to taste
2 eggs beaten with 1/3 cup water
Oil for frying

Sauce
3 tablespoons butter or margarine
3 tablespoons flour
1 cup fish stock
1 cup dry white wine
1/4 teaspoon cumin
Salt and pepper to taste

   Make the sauce: Melt butter in a saucepan over low heat. Stir in flour and mix until smooth. Add fish stock slowly. Add cumin and wine. Simmer for about 10 minutes or until sauce is reduced in volume. Keep warm.
   Dip fish in flour mixed with salt and pepper; shake off excess. Dip in beaten egg and fry in oil until golden. Place on hot platter. Pour sauce over fish and serve.
   Serves 4 to 6.

Baked Whitefish Steaks

6 slices whitefish steaks, 1" thick (about 2 pounds)
1 cup milk
Flour
3 egg yolks beaten with 1/2 cup water and salt and pepper to taste
1/2 cup butter
1/2 cup peanut oil
1/4 cup finely chopped parsley or dill weed

   Soak fish in milk for several hours (or overnight in the refrigerator if fish is frozen). Drain. Dip in flour, then in egg mixture, then in flour.
   Melt butter in a skillet, stir in peanut oil. Sauté fish on both sides until golden but not cooked through. Arrange in a baking pan and bake in a preheated 350° oven for 20 minutes. Dust with parsley or dill. Serve with lemon wedges.
   Serves 6.

   Variation: May substitute carp, sea trout, tuna, salmon steaks, etc.

Fish Fillets in Agristada Sauce

1 1/2 pounds fish fillets
2 large eggs beaten with 1/3 cup water
Flour
Oil for frying
Agristada Sauce (see recipe)

Cut fillets into 3 x 3 squares and dip into beaten egg and then into flour. Fry in medium hot oil until golden brown on both sides. Drain on paper towels, then arrange over warm Agristada Sauce in a shallow dish. Chill. Garnish with parsley sprigs.
Serves 4 to 6.

Variation: Bake a whole fish (about 2 pounds). Pour the hot sauce over all and allow to cool in the refrigerator. Garnish with sprigs of parsley, tomato wedges, and cucumber slices.

Agristada Sauce

1 cup cold water
2 tablespoons flour
2 large eggs
Salt and pepper to taste
Juice of 1 large or 2 small lemons

Place all ingredients (except lemon juice) in a blender and mix until very smooth, or make a paste of flour and water and combine with other ingredients using a wire whisk. Cook very slowly at low to medium heat, stirring constantly until thick. Stir in the lemon juice, drop by drop. Remove from heat and pour into a shallow dish to cool.
Makes about 1 1/4 cups.

Veal Brains in Agristada Sauce I

2 fresh veal brains
1 cup vinegar mixed with 3 cups water
2 eggs beaten with 1/4 cup water
Flour
Oil for sautéeing
1 1/4 cup Agristada Sauce (see recipe)
1/2 cup chopped parsley

Soak brains in vinegar-water for 1 hour. Carefully remove all outer membrane and veins. Wash in cold water, then dip in boiling salted water for about 1 minute. Dry well.

Cut into serving pieces. Dip each piece in the egg mixture, then in the flour. In a frying pan at medium heat, sauté until golden brown on both sides. Arranged on a heated serving dish. Pour sauce over all and sprinkle with chopped parsley. Serve hot.

Serves 6.

Veal Brains in Agristada Sauce II

2 fresh veal brains
3 cups water
1 cup vinegar
1 1/4 cups Agristada Sauce (see recipe)
Chopped parsley

Soak brains in vinegar and water for 1 hour. Carefully remove all outer membrane and veins. Bring a pot of salted water to a boil and add meat; lower heat to medium and simmer 5 minutes. Drain in a colander discarding water. Slice and cool.

Fold meat into hot sauce and spoon into a shallow serving dish. Refrigerate. Sprinkle with chopped parsley and serve cold, accompanied by sliced tomatoes and cucumbers.

Serves 6.

Veal Brains in Brown Sauce

2 fresh veal brains
1 cup vinegar mixed with 3 cups water
1 onion stuck with 1 whole clove
2 egg yolks beaten with 1/3 cup water
Flour
Salt and pepper to taste
3 tablespoons oil
11 tablespoons margarine (pareve)
4 medium potatoes, peeled, quartered, and boiled until tender
2 teaspoons finely chopped dill weed

Soak brains in vinegar-water for 1 hour. Carefully remove all outer membrane and veins. Bring a pot of salted water to a boil; add the meat and onion, and cook gently until tender, about 5 minutes. Drain in a colander. Cut each piece into quarters, dip in egg mixture, and then in flour seasoned with salt and pepper.

Combine oil with 3 tablespoons margarine in a heavy skillet, and sauté meat on both sides until light brown. Remove to a hot serving platter with the boiled potatoes. Add 8 tablespoons margarine to the hot drippings in the skillet and allow to melt and turn brown. Remove from heat and stir in the dill weed. Spoon sauce over all.

Serves 4.

Artichoke, Carrots and Peas

6 artichoke bottoms
3 carrots, sliced in 1/4-inch rounds
Juice of 1 lemon
2 tablespoons peanut or olive oil
3/4 cup fresh green peas

Place all ingredients in a small saucepan. Add water to barely cover. Cook slowly, uncovered, until vegetables are tender. Serve artichoke bottoms topped with carrots and peas. Pour a little sauce over each. Serve as a cold appetizer.

Serves 6.

Lemon Chicken

8 or 9 medium-small potatoes, peeled and quartered
2 1/2 to 3 pound chicken, cut into serving pieces
Paprika

Sauce
1/2 cup olive oil
Juice of 1 lemon
1/4 cup red wine vinegar
2 teaspoons chopped garlic
1 tablespoon each chopped parsley, dill weed, and oregano
1 teaspoon each salt and pepper, or to taste

Combine sauce ingredients in a jar and shake well.

Boil potatoes in salted water until half done; drain. Wash and dry chicken and place in a large bowl with the cooled potatoes. Pour sauce over and marinate for several hours in the refrigerator.

Remove chicken and potatoes from the marinade and arrange in a casserole. Season with paprika. Bake uncovered in a preheated 400° oven for 25 minutes; add remaining marinade and bake 15 minutes or until the potatoes are done and the chicken is brown and tender.

Serves 6 to 8.

Chicken and Lima Beans

3 onions, sliced lengthwise to form crescents
1 tablespoon vegetable oil
2 bunches carrots, peeled and cut into 3-inch sticks
2 1/2 pounds chicken, cut in serving pieces
Salt and pepper to taste
1/2 cup chopped parsley
2 Turkish laurel or bay leaves
2 cups fresh lima beans
1 cup chopped dill weed

In a large pot, sauté onion in oil until soft. Add remaining ingredients (except lima beans and dill). Add water to barely cover chicken and cook slowly until tender. Remove chicken. Add lima beans to stock and cook until tender and liquid almost evaporated. Return chicken to pot, correct seasonings, and add dill. Cook 5 minutes.

Serves 6 to 8.

Bulgarian Chicken

3-pound chicken, cut up
5 potatoes, peeled and cut into walnut-size pieces
4 ripe tomatoes, peeled and cut up
Paprika

Sauce
1/2 cup olive oil
Juice of 1 lemon
3 tablespoons red wine vinegar
2 teaspoons finely chopped garlic
3 tablespoons chopped parsley
1 teaspoon each dried dill and rosemary
Salt and pepper to taste

Place sauce ingredients in a jar and shake well.

Arrange chicken and potatoes in a baking dish. Brush with the sauce. Add tomatoes and dust with paprika over all. Bake, uncovered, in a preheated 350° oven for 20 minutes. Remove from oven and pour on remaining sauce; return to oven for 30 minutes or until potatoes are tender and chicken is golden brown. If potatoes need additional cooking, remove chicken to a platter and continue to cook potatoes until they are soft.

Serves 4 to 6.

Glazed Carrots and Vinegar

1 pound carrots, scraped
4 tablespoons butter or margarine
3 tablespoons chopped dill weed
1/2 teaspoon each salt and pepper
2 to 4 tablespoons red wine vinegar
1 teaspoon finely chopped mint leaves

Cut carrots into sticks 2 inches long. Place in thin layer in a saucepan and add water to barely cover. Add butter and cook uncovered on medium heat until tender, about 25 minutes. Add dill, salt, pepper, vinegar, and mint during last 5 minutes of cooking.

Serves 4 to 6.

Boiled Chicken

1/4 cup olive oil
2 medium onions, sliced lengthwise to form crescents
2 carrots, peeled and sliced into thin rounds
2 celery stalks, sliced thin
Salt and pepper to taste
1 cup chopped parsley
2 large cloves garlic, chopped
1 cup chopped dill weed
3 medium tomatoes, sliced into wedges
2 to 3 pound chicken, cut into serving pieces
3 cups chicken stock or water

In a soup pot, sauté onions in olive oil until soft. Add carrots, celery, salt and pepper and cook until glazed. Stir in parsley, garlic, and dill; continue to cook a few minutes more. Add tomatoes and cook until all the juices are absorbed. Remove the vegetables to a dish.

In the same pot, sauté the chicken pieces on all sides. Return the vegetables to the pot, stir, and add the stock. Cover, lower heat, and cook until the chicken is tender. Remove chicken and vegetables, bring the stock to a boil, and cook 15 minutes to reduce the liquid. Return chicken and vegetables to the pot, heat thoroughly, and transfer to a tureen. Serve hot or at room temperature with fresh crusty bread.

Serve 4 to 6.

Lemon Green Beans

2 medium onions, sliced lengthwise to form crescents
1/4 cup olive oil
1 pound green beans, tips removed
Juice of one lemon
3/4 cup water
Salt and pepper to taste
3 tablespoons chopped parsley

Sauté onions in olive oil until translucent. Add green beans, lemon juice (reserve 1 teaspoon), and water. Cover and cook over low to medium heat, stirring occasionally, until the vegetables are tender. Add salt and pepper, reserved lemon juice, and parsley.

Serves 4 to 6.

Meatballs in Tomato Sauce

1 pound lean ground beef
1 medium onion, finely chopped
1/2 bunch parsley, finely chopped
1/4 cup bread crumbs
2 eggs, slighten beaten
Salt and pepper to taste
Olive oil for frying

Sauce
1/2 cup tomato sauce
1/2 cup water
1/2 bunch parsley, finely chopped (discard stems)
10 cloves garlic, crushed (optional)

    Combine beef, onion, parsley, crumbs, eggs, salt and pepper; shape into fingers 1/2 inch thick and 2 inches long. Fry in oil until brown on both sides. Remove some of the accumulated fat and add sauce ingredients. Cover and simmer until meatballs are cooked through. Serve with vinegar on the side.
    Serves 4.

Pot Roast and Scallions

5 or 6 bunches scallions
Salt and pepper to taste
2 pounds chuck roast
Olive oil for frying
3 large cloves garlic, finely chopped
1/2 cup dry red wine or tomato juice (do not use sherry)
1/2 cup chopped parsley

    Cut scallions into 2-inch pieces. Place in the bottom of a covered roasting pan. Season with salt and pepper.
    Heat olive oil in a frying pan and quickly sear the roast 1 minute on each side, then arrange over the scallions. Add the garlic and wine to the meat juices in the pan; pour over roast. Season with salt and lots of ground pepper.
    Cover pan and bake in a preheated 350° oven for 1 hour or until the meat is tender. Baste four or five times during the baking. Add chopped parsley during the last 15 minutes. Serve hot.
    Serves 6 to 8.

Eggplant Meatballs

1 medium eggplant
3 medium onions, finely chopped
1/4 cup olive oil
1/2 cup tomato sauce
1/2 cup water
1 pound lean ground beef
1/2 cup bread crumbs
1 teaspoon minced garlic
2 large eggs, beaten
Salt and pepper to taste

Prick eggplant, place on cookie sheet and bake in a preheated 375° oven for 30 minutes or until flesh is soft. Cut in half and scrape flesh from skin; mash or chop.

In a large saucepan, sauté onions in olive oil until soft. Stir in tomato sauce and water; lower heat to simmer.

Combine meat, bread crumbs, garlic, eggs, salt and pepper, and shape into walnut-size meatballs. Add to sauce and simmer about 30 minutes or until done. Add the mashed eggplant and simmer 10 minutes. Serve hot.

Serves 4.

Brisket of Beef

4 pounds well-trimmed brisket
1/4 cup olive oil
5 ripe tomatoes, cut up
2 cups tomato sauce
2 onions, sliced
2 Turkish laurel or bay leaves
Salt and pepper to taste
2 teaspoons rosemary

Trim excess fat from meat and brown on all sides in olive oil. Add remaining ingredients and stir a few minutes. Add water to half the height of the meat. Cover pan and roast in a preheated 325° oven for about 2 hours or until meat is tender, basting every half hour.

When the meat has cooled slightly, slice thin and return to the sauce. Serve hot.

Serves 8.

Stuffed Cabbage

1 large head cabbage
2 pounds lean ground beef
1 cup raw rice
1/2 cup chopped parsley
Salt and pepper to taste
1 tablespoon olive oil or vegetable oil
4 large onions, cut lengthwise to form crescents
8-ounce can tomato paste
Juice of one lemon

Bring a large pot of water to the boil; turn off heat and place cabbage in water for 20 minutes or until leaves can be separated easily. Place cabbage in a colander and gently separate the leaves. Save 3 cups of cabbage water.

Combine meat, 1 cup cabbage water, rice, parsley, salt and pepper. Place a heaping-spoonful of mixture at the stem end of the cabbage leaf, turn in sides and roll into a neat package. Squeeze over sink to remove excess water and secure cabbage roll. Repeat until all the meat is used.

Heat olive oil in a large saucepan and sauté onions until soft. Add tomato paste and cook, stirring, a few more minutes; add 1 cup cabbage water and stir. Remove sauce from the pan.

Place a layer of stuffed cabbage rolls in the bottom of the pan and spread with some of the sauce. Repeat until you have several layers of rolls and sauce. Add 1 cup cabbage water and lemon juice. Cover and cook over low heat for 1 hour. Serve with lemon wedges.

Serves about 15.

Dilled Potatoes and Cauliflower

1 head cauliflower
4 medium boiling potatoes, peeled and quartered
1 stick butter or margarine
1/2 cup chopped dill weed

Remove leaves from cauliflower and cut gashes into end of stem. Steam vegetables until just tender; drain. To serve, arrange potatoes around the cauliflower. Add dill to melted butter; spoon over vegetables.

Serves 6.

Pot Roast with Carrots and Tomatoes

2 pounds boneless chuck roast
Flour
1/4 cup olive oil
3 large onions, sliced lengthwise to form crescents
4 garlic cloves, crushed
1 bunch carrots, peeled, cut in half and then lengthwise in fourths
6 ripe tomatoes, cut up
3 Turkish laurel or bay leaves
1 teaspoon paprika
1 teaspoon each salt and pepper
2 1/2 cups beef stock or tomato juice

Roll roast in flour; brown on all sides in olive oil. Remove from pan. Sauté onions in the beef drippings until translucent; add garlic and carrots and sauté lightly. Add tomatoes, bay leaves, paprika, salt, pepper, and beef stock, and stir well.

Return roast to the pot. Cover, lower heat, and cook until tender and the sauce has thickened, about 1 1/2 to 2 hours. Baste during cooking every 20 minutes. Let meat cool 20 minutes before slicing.

To serve, arange the sliced meat on a platter. Gently pile the carrots in a mound in the center and spoon the sauce over the meat and the carrots. Serve hot.

Serves 6 to 8.

Turkish Green Beans

3 onions, sliced lengthwise to form crescents
1/4 cup olive oil
1 1/2 pounds green beans, tips removed
3 ripe tomatoes, cut into wedges
1 cup tomato sauce
1 cup water
Salt and pepper to taste

Sauté onions in olive oil until golden. Add remaining ingredients. Cover and cook on low to medium heat, stirring occasionally, until vegetables are tender.

Serves 6.

Variation: Add 6 small potatoes, peeled and quartered. You can substitute okra for the green beans; remove crown and tips.

Anise Biscotchos

1 cup butter
2 cups sugar
4 large eggs
1/4 teaspoon anise extract
2 teaspoons vanilla extract
1 teaspoon baking powder
3 tablespoons anise seed
5 cups flour

With an electric mixer, cream butter and sugar until smooth. Add eggs one at a time, beating after each addition. Add the anise and vanilla, blending thoroughly. When the batter is light and fluffy, add baking powder and anise seed and mix well. Add flour, one cup at a time, blending after each addition.

Wrap in wax paper and refrigerate 6 to 8 hours. Shape into walnut-size balls and place 2 inches apart on a greased cookie sheet. Bake in a preheated oven at 400°for 15 minutes or until cookies are golden.

Makes 4 dozen.

Fried Semolina Dough

1 1/2 pounds semolina flour (pasta flour)
1/2 teaspoon salt
1 egg
1/3 cup sugar
1 cup oil
1 cake yeast
3/4 cup water
Oil for deep frying
Syrup or confectioners' sugar

Combine ingredients and make a dough the consistency of bread dough. Knead 10 to 15 minutes; cover and let rise 5 hours in a warm place. Knead again and divide into walnut-size balls; cover and let raise again for about 5 hours.

When ready, drop balls into deep hot oil and fry until golden brown. Remove from oil and drain on paper towels. Dip in orange-flavored syrup or roll in confectioners' sugar.

Makes 3 dozen.

Fried Pinwheels and Bow Ties

3 large eggs
2 tablespoons vanilla extract
1/2 cup oil (peanut, walnut, almond, or safflower)
2 1/2 cups flour, sifted
1/2 teaspoon baking powder
6 cups oil for frying
Confectioners' sugar

Syrup
2 cups sugar
1 cup water
Squeeze of lemon juice
Juice of 2 oranges
1/2 teaspoon cinnamon

Combine syrup ingredients (except cinnamon). Cook 15 to 20 minutes until syrup is thick. Add cinnamon and let stand overnight. Syrup can be made ahead and kept on hand.

With an electric mixer, beat eggs, vanilla, and 1/2 cup oil until thick. Add flour sifted with baking powder; knead until smooth. Form into balls the size of an egg. Cover with a towel and allow to rest for 1 hour.

Roll dough paper thin, and cut into 2" x 10" strips. Use a pasta machine if you have one.

For each pinwheel, hold one end of the strip as you submerge the other in medium-hot oil. Place a long-tonged fork into the oil and hook it onto the dough. As you roll the strip onto the fork, keep the pinwheel submerged in the oil. Remove when golden. Place pinwheels on paper towels to drain. Spoon syrup over each pinwheel, sprinkle with confectioners' sugar, and serve warm.

For each bow tie, cut dough into 2" x 5" strips. Pinch strips in center and twist to form bow ties. Fry in medium-hot oil until golden and dust with confectioners' sugar.

Canella (Cinnamon Nut Biscuits)

1/2 cup unsalted butter
1/2 cup white sugar
1/2 cup brown sugar, firmly packed
1 large egg
2 tablespoons heavy cream
1 teaspoon vanilla extract
1 1/2 cups flour
1 teaspoon baking powder
1 1/2 teaspoons cinnamon
1 cup ground walnuts
24 walnut halves
Confectioners' sugar

With an electric mixer, cream butter with white and brown sugar. Add egg, cream, and vanilla. Beat well. Sift together flour, baking powder, and cinnamon, add to butter mixture and blend well. Add ground nuts and mix.

Pinch off walnut-size pieces of dough and roll into balls. Place on a greased cookie sheet. Place a walnut half on each cookie and press to flatten. (Or dough may be rolled into a cigar shape and formed into a crescent on the cookie sheet.)

Bake in a preheated 350° oven about 15 to 20 minutes or until light brown. Dust with confectioners' sugar while still hot.

Makes about 2 dozen.

Walnut or Almond Candy

10 ounces sugar
10 ounces coarsely chopped walnuts or almonds

Melt sugar in a deep pan on low heat, stirring constantly with a wooden spoon. When sugar is melted and golden, quickly remove from heat. Stir in nuts and pour onto a lightly oiled surface.

With oiled hands or protective gloves (be careful — the mixture is very hot!), quickly shape the candy into little balls the size of walnuts. Wrap in plastic wrap or place in tiny paper cases. Store in a tightly covered container.

Makes 2 dozen.

Variation: Substitute 1 cup sesame or poppy seeds for the nuts.

Fried Apples and Apricots

6 ounces dried apricots, chopped
1 3/4 cups boiling water
3 pounds apples, peeled, cored, and quartered
Juice of 1 lemon
3/4 cup unsalted butter, melted
1/2 to 1 cup sugar

In a large pot, soak chopped apricot in the water for 2 hours. Slice apples and add to apricots with the lemon juice. Cook, stirring, until mixture reaches the boil. Lower heat to medium. Cover and cook until apples are soft, about 10 minutes; stir occasionally. Add melted butter and sugar; stir well.

Cook gently for about 15 minutes, stirring occasionally to keep apples from burning. Add more water if necessary. Serve hot or cold.

Makes 1 quart.

Glazed Orange Rinds

3 naval oranges
1 cup strained orange juice (from juice oranges)
1 cup sugar

Cut oranges in half lengthwise and remove the pulp to a bowl. Cut each half-shell into 3 lengthwise pieces. Roll up each slice.

Thread an embroidery needle with size 8 100% cotton thread, doubled. Pierce each rolled-up orange slice through the center and pull onto the thread. When all the coils are threaded, remove needle and tie the ends of the thread together to form a ring. Place in a saucepan and cover with water. Bring to a boil and cook 3 minutes. Change the water and bring to a boil again, repeating 3 or 4 times, until the peel no longer tastes bitter. Discard the water.

Return peels to the pot; add orange juice and sugar. Stir well and simmer uncovered until syrup is reduced to one-third. Cool. Remove thread.

Fill a sterile jar with the peels, add the syrup, and seal the jar. Refrigerate 3 or more days to cure. Serve at room temperature as a dessert. May serve with ice cream.

Makes 18 pieces.

Glazed Grapefruit Rinds: Substitute grapefruit and add 1/2 cup additional sugar to recipe. Use orange juice as indicated, not grapefruit juice.

Candied Orange or Grapefruit Rinds: Cook the rinds at low heat until the syrup evaporates. Hang rings of rinds to dry overnight. Remove thread and place in an airtight container.

Halvah

15-ounce can sesame tahini
2 eggs whites, beaten into stiff peaks
1 cup sliced almonds or pistachios (unsalted)

Syrup
2 cups sugar
1 cup water
1/4 teaspoon vanillin crystals (sold at Greek food stores)
   or 2 teaspoons vanilla

Boil syrup ingredients until very thick, about 15 to 20 minutes (hard ball stage). Cool slightly before using.

With an electric mixer, beat sesame tahini until smooth and creamy and the oil is completely absorbed. Gently fold in egg whites. Mixture will get stiff and pull away from bowl. Slowly add 3/4 cup syrup. Fold in the nuts, then stir in the remaining cup of syrup a little at a time.

Transfer mixture to a loaf pan. Cover and refrigerate for 3 days before unmolding. Will keep for 6 months in refrigerator.

Massapan (Marzipan)

16 ounces blanched slivered almonds
2 egg whites

Syrup
1 cup water
2 cups sugar
Juice of 1/2 lemon
1/8 teaspoon vanillin crystals or 1 teaspoon vanilla extract

Grind almonds finely in a food processor until the mixture begins to stick together slightly. Remove to a large bowl. Beat egg whites until stiff, and gently fold into almonds. Set the mixture aside.

In a deep saucepan combine the syrup ingredients. Bring to boil and cook for about 20 minutes, until very thick and golden in color (hard ball to crack stage). Remove 1 cup hot syrup and fold immediately into the almond mixture; mixing thoroughly. While the candy is soft, return to the food processor and process to a smooth paste. Refrigerate overnight.

The next day, shape spoonfuls of mixture into balls the size of small walnuts. Roll in sugar and place each piece in a tiny paper casing. Allow to air-dry for several days before placing in tightly sealed containers.

Makes 4 dozen.

Syrup and Cherries of Vijna (Sour Cherries)

After Yom Kippur fast, serve drinks made with 2 tablespoons syrup mixed into a glass of cold water.

2 pounds ripe cherries, pitted (save the juice)
2 1/2 pounds sugar
1 cinnamon stick
Juice of 2 lemons
2 cups water

Combine cherries, cherry juice, sugar, and cinnamon stick. Stir and allow to macerate overnight, about 12 hours.

Remove the cinnamon stick, add water, and cook on low to medium heat for 20 minutes, skimming the surface occasionally. Add lemon juice. Bring to a boil and cook 10 minutes.

Remove cherries and place in a sterilized 16-ounce jar. Refrigerate. Meanwhile, continue cooking the syrup another 5 to 10 minutes, then pour into a hot, sterilized 16-ounce bottle and refrigerate.

Violet Syrup

4 cups freshly picked, unsprayed fragrant violets
2 cups boiling water
6 cups sugar
Juice of 1/2 lemon
2 cups water

Select only the freshest and the most unblemished violets in your garden.

Place violet petal in a deep bowl and pour the boiling water over them. Weight down with a heavy dish to keep them submerged. Place the bowl in a draft-free place at room temperature for 24 hours.

Line a colander with layers of rinsed cheesecloth, and place over a bowl. Pour violets and liquid into the colander, squeezing out juice from the violets; discard violets.

Place sugar, lemon juice, and water in a saucepan and boil into a very thick syrup, near the candy stage. Add violet water and bring to a rolling boil. Boil 10 minutes or until thickened. Pour into sterile bottles. Allow to cool, then seal and refrigerate. Serve with ice water or club soda.

Makes 2 quarts.

Variation: Substitute 4 cups fragrant red rose petals and add 1 cinnamon stick per bottle of syrup.

Almond Syrup

4 1/2 cups water
20 ounces ground blanched almonds
6 to 7 cups sugar
3 tablespoons bitter almond extract
Juice of 2 oranges

Bring water to a boil; add almonds and return to a boil. Remove from heat and allow to cool thoroughly. Squeeze the ground almonds in several layers of rinsed cheesecloth.

Pour almond liquid into a saucepan; add sugar, bitter almond extract, and orange juice. Stir well and bring to a boil; cook to a thick syrup consistency. Let cool completely. If the syrup is not thick enough, boil again for 5 minutes.

Pour into sterile bottles, seal, and refrigerate. Can be used immediately. Serve with ice water or with club soda.

Makes 1 quart.

Mint Syrup

8 cups fresh mint leaves, chopped
2 1/2 cups boiling water
8 cups sugar
3 cups water
Green food coloring
3 tablespoons mint essential oil or extract

Place the chopped mint leaves in a crock or a deep bowl; add boiling water. Place a flat dish over the leaves and weight it down. Allow to stand overnight.

Bring sugar and 3 cups water to a boil and cook 10 to 15 minutes. Meanwhile, squeeze the juice from the mint leaves; add mint juice to the syrup, bring to a boil, cook 5 minutes and remove from heat. Discard leaves. Add green food color to make the syrup a bright green. Add the mint oil and stir.

Pour into sterile bottles. Refrigerate. Syrup is ready to use.

Almond Cooler

2 tablespoons almond syrup (see recipe)
2 tablespoons yogurt
6 ounces cold water

Combine all ingredients and chill. Serves 1.

Grenadine Syrup

4 pomegranates, quartered
3/4 cup sugar per cup of fruit juice
Juice of lemon
2 teaspoon vanilla extract
1 cinnamon stick per jar of syrup

Combine pomegranate juice, sugar, and lemon juice in a saucepan and bring to a boil. Cook until the sugar clarifies and begins to thicken, about 15 minutes; add the vanilla and cook 5 minutes longer. Allow to cool overnight.

The next day, bring to a boil and cook 5 to 10 minutes to thicken. Pour into sterilized bottles, seal, and refrigerate. Serve with ice water or club soda.

Make 1 1/2 quarts.

Turkish Coffee

4 heaping teaspoons Turkish coffee (espresso may be substituted)
4 teaspoons sugar
4 demitasse cups water

Combine coffee, sugar, and water in a brass librik or other small pan. Bring to a boil and remove from heat; do this three times. Pour into demitasse cups and drizzle a little ice water on coffee surface to settle the grounds.

Serves 4.

Variation 1: Add a little powdered cardamon or cinnamon to coffee before serving.

Variation 2: In a double boiler, beat by hand 1 large egg with 4 tablespoons sugar. Cook until it becomes a creamy pale yellow high whip. Add 1 teaspoon rum, cognac or kirsh. Spoon onto surface of coffee.

Uncle Joseph Finzi with his mother circa 1890.

Benaroya family in Bulgaria, 1932.

Vaëssa cousins at a party in Lyon.

Mother and friends at her 20th birthday celebration. Geneva.

Sunday Morning Bread Making

On Sundays my grandparents awoke at dawn, ate a breakfast of bread, butter, homemade jam, and Turkish coffee, and prepared to bake the week's supply of bread. They treasured Sunday morning as a time to catch up on each other's thoughts.

Grandfather plunged his huge, roughened hands into the flour bin and began making the yeasty bread that Grandmother filled with mixtures of cheese, spinach, eggplant, or zucchini for the Sunday afternoon outing.

A small window opened from their kitchen into the apartment's entrance hall. Aromas from the window greeted me as soon as I arrived at Rue du Terreaux du Temple. I raced up the marble stairs that spiraled six floors or took the tiny glass elevator, whichever would get me upstairs faster. When I opened the door I heard laughter and singing in Ladino because, although they each spoke five languages, it was always Ladino on Sunday morning.

Grandmother waited until I arrived to "read" the coffee grounds. She ceremoniously swirled her coffee cup and turned it upside down in the saucer. As the grounds took shape, she read her future. If the grounds took the shape of a dog, this meant faithfulness in marriage. A square shape meant that she would receive good news; a house meant a reunion; a road meant travel; a mountain meant a change in business; and a fish meant money. Grandfather looked amused as I listened to Grandmother's forecasting.

Later, when my cousins arrived, Grandmother sent us running back and forth to various houses where food for the day's outing was being prepared. Not everyone in the family had a telephone, so our job was to keep everyone informed about the food's readiness.

The following breads were taken on summer picnics.

Bulgarian Filled Bread

6 cups unbleached flour
1/3 cup olive oil
1 teaspoon salt
1/4 cup sugar
3 large eggs
2 yeast cakes
1 1/2 cups warm milk
2 egg yolks, beaten
Grated kaseri or Swiss cheese

In a large bowl combine flour, oil, salt, sugar, and eggs. Crumble yeast over the mixture and add warm milk. Mix thoroughly until the dough pulls away from the sides of the bowl. It will be slightly sticky.

Knead on floured surface for 15 minutes (dough should be easy to knead). Return to bowl and cover with a clean towel. Let rise in a warm place, free from draft, until double in bulk (about 2 hours); punch down and let rise until double. Punch down and divide into 4 equal parts.

Generously oil two 9-or 10-inch round baking pans or springform pans, 3 1/2 inches deep. Roll out two pieces of dough and press each into the bottom of a pan, spreading it evenly with your fingertips. Cover each with half the filling. Cut each of the two remaining pieces of dough into 6 equal strips and place them evenly over the filling, as if they were spokes of a wheel, to let steam escape during baking. Brush tops with beaten egg yolk and sprinkle with grated cheese. Allow to rest 15 minutes.

Bake in a preheated 350° oven for 1 hour or until top is golden brown. Remove from pan and cool on rack before slicing. Bread will keep for several days in refrigerator (slice and serve at room temperature or warm).

Makes 2. Each loaf serves 8.

Basic Cheese Filling
1/2 pound farmers cheese
1 pound kaseri cheese or Swiss cheese, grated
1/2 pound feta cheese, finely crumbled (optional)
1 teaspoon garlic, finely chopped (optional)
1 teaspoon each salt and pepper (correct seasoning to taste)
3 large eggs, beaten

Combine all ingredients. Makes enough for two loaves of filled bread.

Spinach Filling

To the Basic Cheese Filling, add (a) two 10-ounce packages chopped spinach that have been thawed and squeezed completely dry, or (b) 1 pound fresh, finely chopped spinach leaves (uncooked), with stems removed, well washed and dried.

Zucchini Filling

To the Basic Cheese Filling, omit salt and add 6 slender zucchini (coarsely grated, salted, allowed to stand for 30 minutes, and squeezed dry) and 3 medium onions (finely chopped and sautéed in olive oil or vegetable oil until translucent).

Eggplant Filling

To the Basic Cheese Filling, add 3 medium onions (finely chopped and sautéed in a little olive or vegetable oil until translucent) and 1 to 2 pounds slender eggplant (baked whole in preheated 375° oven for 25 minutes or until soft, cut in half, and flesh scraped from skin and mashed until smooth).

Challah Crowns

5 cups unbleached flour
1 teaspoon salt
1/3 cup sugar
1/4 cup peanut oil
2 eggs plus 1 yolk
2 yeast cakes
1 1/2 cups warm milk
2 egg yolks, beaten, for glazing

In a large bowl, combine flour, salt, and sugar. Add oil, eggs, and egg yolk. Crumble the yeast over the mixture and add the milk, a little at a time, mixing thoroughly. If dough is too sticky, add a little more flour and mix until the dough pulls away from the sides of the bowl.

Place on a floured surface and knead in another cup of flour; knead for 15 minutes or until smooth and elastic. Dough should be easy to knead. Return dough to the bowl and cover with a clean towel. Place in warm, draft-free place to rise for 1 1/2 hours.

Divide dough in half, and cut each part into three equal pieces. Roll each into a rope; braid ropes and shape into rings on greased baking pans. Let rise for 30 minutes. Brush with beaten egg yolk. Bake in a preheated 350° oven for 40 minutes or until golden brown.

Makes 2 loaves.

Borekas

7 cups unsifted flour
1 1/2 cups peanut oil or light vegetable oil
2 cups hot water
Filling (use filling from Cheese Filled Coils, Eggplant Pie,
    or Spinach Turnovers)
Egg yolks
Oil

In a large bowl, place flour, peanut oil, and 1 cup water and mix with your hands. Add remaining water and mix, but do not knead or overmix; the dough is ready when it pulls away from the sides of the bowl. (You may need to use a little flour to remove dough from your hands.) Cover dough with a clean towel and allow to rest for 30 minutes. Do not refrigerate.

Dust work surface and a rolling pin with flour. Pinch off a piece of dough the size of an egg and roll out into a circle about 5 inches in diameter. Place a heaping teaspoon of filling in the center and fold circle in half to form a half moon. Gently press down edges. Trim by firmly pressing the rim of a large drinking glass over the boreka and removing excess dough. Seal by pressing all around the cut edge and imprinting with the tines of a fork.

Generously oil the surface of a shallow baking pan. Brush the tops and bottoms of the borekas with oil as you place them in the baking pan. Brush tops with beaten egg yolk to glaze. You can sprinkle the spinach borekas with sesame seeds and the cheese borekas with grated cheese. The eggplant borekas are left plain. Bake in a preheated 450° oven until golden and puffy, about 25 to 30 minutes. Serve hot or at room temperature.

Makes 3 dozen.

Variation: Add 1 cup grated kaseri or Swiss cheese to the flour, and increase peanut oil to 2 cups. Salt to taste.

Note: Cooked borekas can be frozen after they have cooled. To reheat, place frozen borekas in a preheated 350° oven for 20 minutes or until hot.

Meat Pastel (Savory Meat Pie)

Boreka dough (see recipe)

Filling
1 1/2 pounds lean ground beef
3 medium onions, sliced lengthwise to form crescents
1/2 pound mushrooms, chopped
1/2 teaspoon coriander or rosemary (optional)
1 tablespoon finely chopped garlic
1 teaspoon each salt and pepper
3 1/2 tablespoons flour
1/4 cup dry red wine or water
3 large eggs
1/4 cup oil (approx.)
1 egg yolk, lightly beaten

Prepare boreka dough. Cover bowl with a towel and set aside while making filling.

In a large frying pan, sauté meat until brown, stirring constantly. Remove from pan. Cook onions in beef fat and juices until translucent; remove from heat and drain fat.

Combine beef, onions, mushrooms, coriander, garlic, salt, and pepper and stir well. Add flour mixed with wine, and eggs; blend well and set aside.

Divide dough into two parts, one a third larger than the other. With a rolling pin, roll out the larger piece and place in a well-greased 8 x 12 x 2 baking pan so that dough hangs over the side about 1 inch all around. Spoon filling into shell, spreading evenly. Gently fold the overhanging dough over the filling.

Roll out the smaller piece of dough to about 1 inch larger than the pan. Place over the filled shell and tuck the edges down between the pan and the pie. Generously brush the top with oil and lightly beaten egg yolk.

Cut 3 to 4 steam holes in the center of the pie with a knife. Bake in a preheated 350° oven for 50 to 60 minutes until golden brown. Remove from oven and let cool in pan. Serve warm or at room temperature.

Serves 8 to 16.

Sesame Flat Bread Rings

5 1/2 to 6 cups unbleached white flour
4 tablespoons oil
3 tablespoons sugar
1 tablespoon salt
3 packages dry yeast
2 1/2 cups warm water (120°F. - 130°F.)
1 egg beaten with 2 tablespoons water
Sesame seeds

In a large bowl, combine flour, oil, sugar, and salt. Sprinkle yeast over mixture and pour in the warm water. Mix thoroughly. The dough should pull away from the sides of the bowl in a soft ball. Turn onto a floured surface, cover with a clean towel, and let rest for 10 minutes.

Knead the dough for 15 to 20 minutes until it is smooth and elastic. Place in an oiled bowl and cover the surface with a little oil. Cover bowl with a towel and place in a warm place to rise until doubled, about 2 hours. Remove dough from bowl and punch down.

Knead 5 to 10 minutes, then divide into 16 pieces. Roll each piece into a rope, then form a ring, 6 to 8 inches in diameter and 1/4-inch thick. Brush with egg mixture and coat with sesame seeds. Place on a greased baking sheet and bake in a preheated 350° oven for 25 minutes. Bread will rise slightly during baking. Cool on racks.

Makes 16 rings.

Fried Yeast Dough

1 package dry yeast
3/4 cup lukewarm water
3 tablespoons sugar
1/8 teaspoon salt
3 1/2 cups flour
1 teaspoon baking soda
1 tablespoon cinnamon
2 eggs, beaten
2 tablespoons oil
Oil for deep frying
Orange syrup (see recipe)
Ground pistachios

Sprinkle yeast in water, add sugar and salt; stir and set aside 15 minutes. Sift together 3 cups flour, baking soda, and cinnamon. Make a well; add the yeast mixture, eggs, and oil. Stir into a dough and turn out onto a well-floured surface and knead the last 1/2 cup flour into the dough. Continue to knead the dough until smooth (10 to 15 minutes).

Return to bowl; cover and place in a warm place to rise until double (2 hours). Punch down and knead 5 minutes; pinch off walnut-size pieces of dough; roll each in flour. Cover and allow to rise one more time, about 1 1/2 hours.

Drop into hot oil in a deep fryer. Fry until golden brown; remove to a colander and drain excess oil. Soak in hot syrup a few minutes.

Arrange on a serving dish so that each level is smaller than the one below; as it gets higher until there is one on top of the mountain. Drizzle more syrup over the cakes. Sprinkle with ground pistachios.

Serves 15.

My mother, Daouda Benaroya, with my father, Isaac Alchech, sharing their wedding day with their cousins Chorine Vaëssa and Joseph Sultani. Geneva, May 22, 1943.

My brother, Jacques, and I, 1950.

Aunt Mimi, my mother holding me and Grandmother holding Jacques in front of the family lingerie store in Geneva, 1947.

My brother and I, 1949.

Here I am with my intended, Michel Sultani.

I am in front of the Brunswick Monument Park. Geneva, 1948.

Grandmother Mathilde Alchech, Jacques, and I on the Pont du Mont Blanc. Geneva, 1953.

Desayuno

Desayuno means "breakfast" in Spanish, but to Sephardic Jews the desayuno means a particular kind of meal, usually served on the Sabbath or Holy Days. Our family served the desayuno whenever we needed a quick meal, because all the foods were usually on hand.

If, for example, we were busy preparing for a holiday, Grandmother would send us scurrying around the kitchen or into the storage closets to gather spiced fruit, jams, borekas, olives, cheeses, and hard boiled eggs. Meanwhile, she quickly made a fritada with the zucchini or leeks that she had left from le marché.

I was particularly pleased with meals like these because they were relaxed and informal, and we could pick up many of the foods with our fingers. Actually the meals were more like picnics, which made them the grandchildrens' favorite.

I was proud watching everyone enjoy the yogurt because I had helped make it. When I was eight years old, Grandfather began sending me with a milk pail to the dairy a few blocks away. The place smelled sweet and warm, and the milk containers stood taller than I did. The dairy man filled my pail with creamy raw milk and gave me a piece of cheese to eat on the way home.

When I returned, Grandfather poured the milk into a pot and heated it until it boiled. As the milk cooled, he removed the film that formed on top, which we ate sprinkled with sugar. Then we prepared the yogurt and poured it into the glasses that Grandmother had set out on a tray. Grandfather put the yogurt in the unlit oven. I tucked blankets around the oven door to keep the drafts out.

The next day the fresh yogurt was ready to eat with Grandmother's wonderful raspberry jam. I loved the contrast between the rosy jam and the sweet white custard.

Yaourt (Yogurt)

1/2 gallon whole milk
8 ounces heavy cream (whipping cream)
10 tablespoons commercial yogurt

Stir milk and cream together and bring to a boil. Immediately remove from heat and allow to cool to 110° (or until you can easily put your fingers in the milk and count to 10). Add the yogurt and stir well with a wire whisk.

Pour into nine 8-ounce cups and cover with clean towels to keep out drafts. Place in unlit oven or other warm place (90°to 120°). Let stand undisturbed for 10 hours, until mixture is firm when gently shaken. Refrigerate.

Dill Cheese

2 cups yogurt
1 teaspoon very finely chopped garlic
1 teaspoon salt
1/3 cup finely chopped dill weed, parsley, shallots, or scallions

Spread double layer of cheesecloth in a bowl. Combine all ingredients and pack into the cheesecloth; bring up the corners and tie the neck off with a rubber band. Hang over the sink or a bowl to drip excess liquid.

The next day, squeeze the cheese ball very gently by gripping the neck with one hand and twisting the ball with the other (do not allow the cheese to come through the cheesecloth). Hang over the sink one more day before removing from cheesecloth. Cheese will be dry and creamy.

Place in a covered container and refrigerate immediately. Serve at room temperature with crisp crackers or toast, sliced carrots, celery stick, tomato wedges, cucumber slices, etc.

Makes 10 ounces.

Herbed Cheese

1 cup cottage cheese or grated farmers cheese
1 cup yogurt
1 teaspoon each chopped dill, scallions, and parsley
1 teaspoon finely chopped garlic or shallots
Salt and pepper to taste

Combine all ingredients. Serve with tomato wedges, cucumbers, black olives, and a variety of crusty breads, such as black bread, French bread, or Italian bread.

Peppered Eggs

2 tomatoes, chopped
2 green peppers, chopped
Vegetable oil for sautéing
Black pepper
6 eggs, beaten

Sauté vegetables in a little oil until soft. Add black pepper to make mixture spicy. Add eggs and cook until eggs are set.
Serves 2 to 3.

Eggs and Tomatoes

Olive oil, butter, or margarine
Sliced tomatoes
Swiss cheese, grated
Eggs
Salt and pepper to taste

Heat a little olive oil in a frying pan. Arrange tomatoes on bottom of pan. Cover with cheese. Crack eggs over cheese. Season with salt and pepper. Cover pan and cook on low heat until the eggs are set and yolks are still liquid.

Vegetable Omelet

1 cup each coarsely chopped onions, green bell peppers, and tomatoes
Oil for sautéing
6 eggs, beaten
1 cup grated kaseri or Swiss cheese
Salt and pepper to taste
Butter or margarine for frying

Sauté onions and peppers in oil until soft. Add tomatoes and cook for 2 minutes. Combine vegetables, eggs, cheese, salt and pepper. Melt butter in a frying pan; add egg mixture and cook, covered, at medium heat until eggs are set and puffy. Serve immediately.

Serves 4.

Variation: Add 1 cup coarsely grated zucchini, lightly salted and squeezed dry, to the egg mixture.

Potato Omelet

2 1/2 pounds boiling potatoes
2 large onions, sliced lengthwise to form crescents
Oil for sautéing
5 eggs, beaten
Handful of chopped parsley
Salt and pepper to taste
4 tablespoons margarine

Boil potatoes until just tender. When cool, peel and slice. Sauté onions in a little oil until soft. Combine potatoes, onions, eggs, parsley, salt and pepper.

Melt margarine in large frying pan. Add egg mixture; cover and cook over low to medium heat. When the bottom is brown, slide omelet onto a plate that is slightly larger than the omelet. Turn pan on top of omelet and invert omelet so that you can cook other side. (If you don't think you can manage inverting the omelet, bake in a 350° oven until top is light brown.) Cut omelet in wedges and serve with tomato wedges and sliced cucumbers.

Serves 6 to 8.

Fruit Omelet I

2 cups fruit (peaches, apricots, plums, blueberries, pears, or cherries, in any combination)
4 tablespoons unsalted butter
4 eggs, beaten
1 teaspoon vanilla
1/2 teaspoon cinnamon
Sugar
Yogurt

Peel fruit and cut into small pieces. Sauté in 2 tablespoons butter; combine with beaten eggs, vanilla, and cinnamon. Fry omelet in remaining butter on both sides until golden. Serve with a dusting of sugar and a dollop of yogurt.
Serves 2 to 4.

Fruit Omelet II

2 apples, peeled, cored, and chopped
2 medium peaches, peeled, pitted, and chopped (may use apricots)
1/2 cup pitted cherries, cut in half
6 tablespoons butter
Juice of 1 orange
1/4 teaspoon cinnamon
4 teaspoons sugar
4 eggs
1/2 cup milk

Sauté fruit in 4 tablespoons butter for 2 minutes. Add orange juice, cinnamon, and sugar and cook until mixture softens.

Beat eggs with milk. In another pan, heat 2 tablespoons butter. Add eggs, lower heat, and cover; cook until omelet is set and double in size. Slide omelet onto a plate, spread with half the fruit, and fold in half. Cover with remaining fruit.
Serves 4.

Baked Zucchini

4 narrow zucchini, about 6 inches long
Salt
3 large eggs, beaten
1 cup feta cheese, crumbled
1 1/4 cup grated Swiss or kaseri cheese
3 tablespoons flour
3 tablespoons finely chopped parsley
Salt and pepper to taste

Grate zucchini coarsely and place in a colander. Sprinkle with salt, stir, and let stand 5 to 10 minutes. Squeeze out liquid. Rinse with water to remove the salt, and squeeze very dry.

Combine zucchini, eggs, feta cheese, 1 cup Swiss cheese, flour, parsley, salt and pepper, and pour into a lightly oiled casserole. Sprinkle with remaining cheese and bake in a preheated 350° oven until golden, about 1 hour.

Serves 6.

Variation: Substitute 2 1/2 cups chopped leeks or 2 1/2 cups cooked, chopped, well-drained spinach for the zucchini.

Broccoli Souffle

3 to 5 cups finely chopped broccoli
2 large eggs, beaten
2 cups small curd cottage cheese
1 1/2 cups kaseri or Swiss cheese, grated
Salt and pepper to taste

Dry vegetables thoroughly. Combine all ingredients and place in a greased baking dish. Bake 45 minutes in a preheated 350° oven.

Serves 2 to 4.

Variations. Any of the following vegetables may be substituted for the broccoli: cauliflower (3 to 5 cups finely chopped), celery or leeks (3 to 5 cups cut in 1-inch pieces and simmered in water until tender), zucchini (3 to 5 cups coarsely grated), fresh spinach (1 pound finely chopped), or the flesh of a baked eggplant. You may use crumbled feta cheese instead of kaseri.

Poached Eggs in Creamed Spinach

3 pounds fresh spinach
4 tablespoons butter
2 1/4 cups cold milk
1/2 teaspoon each salt and pepper
1 teaspoon finely chopped garlic (optional)
3 tablespoons flour
4 extra-large eggs

Wash spinach and remove stems; dry between layers of paper towels. Chop medium-fine.

In a saucepan, combine butter, 3/4 cup milk, salt and pepper and cook on low heat until the butter is melted. Add spinach all at once and stir. Cover and cook 3 to 5 minutes, stirring occasionally. Add garlic. Continue to cook uncovered for about 5 minutes or until very little liquid remains.

Stir or whisk flour and remaining milk into a smooth mixture. Add to the spinach and continue to cook, stirring, until the mixture is thickened and creamy, about 5 to 10 minutes.

Makes four evenly-spaced hollows in the creamed spinach and crack an egg into each. Be careful not to break the yolks. Gently cover with the surrounding spinach. Cover pan and simmer for 3 to 5 minutes at low heat until eggs are done (whites should be firm and yolks liquid). Serve over mashed potatoes.

Serves 4.

Poached Egg Salad

2 thin cucumbers, peeled and sliced in rounds (use seedless cucumbers
   if available)
1 tablespoon salt
4 ripe tomatoes, peeled and sliced in wedges
1 medium onion, finely chopped
5 tablespoons olive oil
4 poached eggs, cooled to room temperature
1 tablespoon finely chopped parsley

Salt the cucumbers; toss and allow to stand 15 minutes. Combine tomatoes and onions in a shallow serving dish. Rinse and drain cucumbers; combine with tomatoes and onions. Drizzle olive oil over and toss. Adjust seasoning. Place poached eggs on top of salad and sprinkle with parsley.

Serves 4.

Borekitas

Dough
1 cup vegetable oil
1/2 cup water
1/2 teaspoon salt
1/2 cup grated Swiss or kaseri cheese
3 to 4 cups flour

   In a large bowl, combine oil, water, salt, and cheese and mix well. Add flour gradually until a soft dough is formed. Let rest 10 to 15 minutes.
   Select filling and combine ingredients.
   Pinch off a ball of dough the size of a small egg. Very gently, flatten and roll into a round 4 inches in diameter. Place a level tablespoons of filling in the center. Fold the dough over the filling to form a half moon. Seal the edges shut by pressing down all the way around the curved edge, then form into a puffy crescent.
   Place on an oiled baking sheet. Sprinkle with additional grated cheese, and bake for about 35 minutes in a preheated 350° oven until golden brown. Serve at room temperature.

Cheese filling
2 cups shredded Swiss or kaseri cheese
2 large eggs, beaten
1/2 teaspoon finely chopped garlic
1/4 cup finely chopped parsley
Salt and pepper to taste

Spinach filling
2 cups finely chopped fresh spinach leaves
2 large eggs, beaten
1/2 teaspoon finely chopped garlic (optional)
1 cup shredded Swiss or kaseri cheese
Salt and pepper to taste

Eggplant filling
1 1/2 cup mashed, cooked eggplant flesh
1/2 cup finely chopped onion, sauteed
1 cup shredded Swiss or kaseri cheese
2 large eggs, beaten
Salt and pepper to taste

Potato filling
2 cups mashed potatoes
1/2 cup finely chopped onions, sauteed
2 large eggs, beaten
1 cup shredded Swiss or kaseri cheese
1/4 cup finely chopped parsley or dill
Salt and pepper to taste

Rice Pudding

1 cup raw white rice
3 cups water
3 cups milk
1/2 cup sugar
1 egg yolk
1/2 teaspoon vanilla
1 teaspoon cinnamon
1/2 cup chopped nuts (optional)

Add rice to boiling water and cook uncovered until the water is absorbed. Add milk and sugar. Cover and cook on low heat until most of the milk is absorbed. Add egg yolk and vanilla and continue cooking, uncovered, until creamy. Sprinkle top with cinnamon and chopped nuts.
Serves 8.

Variation: Use 3 cups water instead of 3 cups milk.

Semolina Pudding

2 cups milk
1/3 cup semolina or farina
5 tablespoons sugar
1/4 cup ground walnuts, almonds, or hazelnuts
1 teaspoon cinnamon

Bring milk to scalding point. Slowly add semolina, stirring constantly. Lower heat, add sugar, and cook until thickened, continuing to stir. Pour into bowls. Top with nuts and cinnamon or sliced summer fruits. Serve at room temperature.
Serves 4.

Almond Custard

1 cup Almond Milk (see recipe)
1/2 cup sugar
1 cup water or milk
1 envelope unflavored gelatin
1/2 cup potato starch
2 eggs

Combine all ingredients in a blender and mix well. Cook over low heat, stirring constantly, until thickened. This stage will be reached when custard comes to a boil. Pour into a bowl and refrigerate. Serve with fruit and cookies.
Serves 4.

Almond Milk

20 ounces chopped blanched almonds
3 to 4 cups water

Grind almonds into a meal in a blender or food processor. Place in a saucepan and cover with water. Bring to a boil; cook 10 minutes. Let cool, then strain liquid into a bowl through several layers of rinsed cheesecloth. Squeeze to remove all liquid from almonds.

Use for making almond syrups and custards. Reserve the almonds for making candy (see recipe for almond candy).

Sweet Borekitas

3 1/4 cups unsifted flour
1/2 cup oil
1/4 cup sugar
1 cup hot water
1 cup butter or margarine, melted
Oil
1 egg yolk
Orange syrup (see recipe)

Filling 1
1 cup ground almonds
Grated zest of 1 lemon
1 tablespoon cinnamon
1/4 teaspoon powdered cloves
1/2 cup sugar

Filling 2
1 cup ground walnuts
Grated zest of 1 orange
1 tablespoon cinnamon
1/4 teaspoon nutmeg
1/2 cup sugar

In a large bowl, place flour, oil, sugar, and hot water and mix quickly with your hands until dough is blended and pulls away from the sides of the bowl. Do not knead or overmix. Rub excess dough off your hands over the bowl of dough. Lightly press dough into a ball. Cover bowl and allow to rest at room temperature for 1 hour.

Select filling and combine ingredients.

Pinch off pieces of dough the size of an egg and roll into circles 5 inches in diameter. Place a tablespoon of filling in the center, drizzle with 1 teaspoon melted butter, and fold circle over filling to form a half moon. Gently press down edges. Trim dough by pressing the rim of a large glass firmly over the borekita and removing excess. Using the tines of a fork, seal by pressing and imprinting all the way around the cut edge.

Brush with oil and place in a well-oiled baking pan. Brush with egg yolk and bake at 350° until golden, about 30 minutes. Remove from oven and dip immediately in hot orange syrup.

Apricot Syrup

1 pound ripe apricots, pits removed
1 1/4 pounds sugar
Juice of 1 lemon
1 1/2 cups water or fruit juice
1/2 stick cinnamon

Cut up apricots and combine with other ingredients. Allow to macerate about 12 hours or overnight.

Remove cinnamon stick. Bring mixture to a boil; reduce heat and cook for 20 minutes, skimming the surface occasionally. Drain fruit into a bowl, returning liquid to pan. Bring to a boil and simmer for 15 minutes. Refrigerate (may be combined with fruit, if desired).

Serve syrup plain or with its fruit over ice cream, cake, yogurt, eggs, pancakes, etc.

Note: Recipe may be multiplied as desired. Other fruits in season, such as peaches, plums, berries, oranges, or lemons, may be substituted.

Fresh Prunes

1 pound purple Italian prunes, or red, yellow, or purple plums
1 cup sugar
Juice of 2 lemons

Pit fruit and cut prunes in half, or plums in quarters. Place in a pot and barely cover with water. Add sugar and lemon juice; stir well. Bring to a boil and cook uncovered at medium heat until the fruit is tender and the liquid is almost gone. Chill.

Serves 6.

Fruit Compote

2 pounds fruit: peaches, nectarines, plums, apricots, cherries, or apples
1 cup water
1/4 cup sugar (approx.)
Juice of 1 lemon
1 cinnamon stick, broken in half

Prepare fruit by peeling, removing pits, and/or cutting into serving size pieces.

Combine water, sugar (amount depends upon sweetness of fruit), lemon juice, and cinnamon and bring to a boil. Add fruit and simmer, uncovered, stirring occasionally, until fruit is soft. Serve cold.

Variation: Use any 3 fruits in combination. Sauté in 3 tablespoons butter before adding other ingredients.

Candied Fruit

2 1/2 pounds fruit: pears, peaches, apricots, plums, or quinces, etc. (do not
    combine)
2 cups sugar
2 teaspoons cinnamon
1 teaspoon cardamon
Juice of 1 orange
1 teaspoon grated orange zest
1 teaspoon grated lemon zest

Combine all ingredients and macerate in refrigerator overnight.

Bring mixture to a boil; lower heat and simmer for 20 minutes or until syrup is very thick. Stir gently and often. Fill hot, sterile jars three-fourths full with fruit and cover with syrup. Follow standard canning process or store in refrigerator or freezer. (Contact your county extension office home economist or consult USDA bulletin #56 for complete and safe canning instructions.)

Serve chilled, or remove each piece carefully and roll in sugar.

Makes 1 quart.

Preserved Figs

2 pounds unpeeled Calimyrna figs
3 cups sugar
2 cups water
Juice of 1/2 lemon
1 vanilla bean

With a scissors, cut stems from figs; discard. Combine sugar and water in a pot; boil 15 minutes. Add figs, lemon juice, and vanilla bean. Boil 15 to 20 minutes. Remove from heat and allow to cool.

Pour into sterilized jars (do not cut the vanilla bean and release the seeds into the syrup). Follow standard canning process or store in refrigerator or freezer. (Contact your county extension office home economist or consult USDA bulletin #56 for complete and safe canning instructions.)

Makes two quarts.

Orange Marmalade

4 juice oranges
5 cups sugar
Juice of 4 lemons

Cut oranges into quarters and remove the flesh. Cut the peels into extremely thin strips and place in a large pot; cover with cold water and bring to a boil. Boil for 1 minute and discard the water, repeating the process 3 or more times until the peels no longer taste bitter. Drain.

Slice the orange flesh very thin and stir into the pot with the boiled rinds, sugar, and lemon juice. Bring to a rolling boil, lower heat and, stirring occasionally, cook for 20 to 30 minutes until the sugar is transparent and very thick. Rinds should be heavily glazed. Skim surface of jam from time to time during cooking.

Pour into hot sterilized jars. Follow standard canning process or store in refrigerator or freezer. (Contact your county extension office home economist or consult USDA bulletin #56 for complete and safe canning instructions.)

Makes four 8-ounce jars.

Preserved Cherries

2 pounds ripe red or black cherries, pitted
3 1/4 cups sugar
1 cup water
Juice of 1/2 lemon
1/2 stick cinnamon per jar of preserves (optional)

In a large pot, bring the sugar and water to a boil. Boil 15 minutes from the time the syrup reaches a boil. Add cherries and boil 15 minutes. The syrup should be thick, smooth, and shiny. If the syrup looks too loose, cook 10 to 25 minutes more. Follow standard canning process or store in refrigerator or freezer. (Contact your county extension office home economist or consult USDA bulletin #56 for complete and safe canning instructions.)

Makes four 8-ounce jars.

Quince Marmalade

3 red-skinned apples
3 cups water
4 medium-size ripe quince, quartered
Sugar (1 cup for each cup grated quince)
Juice of 2 lemons
Cinnamon (1/2 stick for each jar)

Peel and core apples and quince. Place peel and cores in a saucepan with the water (save apples for another recipe). Bring to a boil; reduce heat to medium and cook until the liquid has been reduced by half. Coarsely grate the quince into a measuring cup.

Drain the apple-quince liquid through a sieve into a bowl and discard peel and cores. Return liquid to pan; add sugar, lemon juice, and grated quince. Bring to a boil, then reduce heat to medium and cook gently until the quince is tender and the mixture is thickened, about 20 to 30 minutes. Stir occasionally. Skim the surface of the jam as needed.

Remove from heat and pour into sterilized jars, adding 1/2 stick cinnamon to each jar. Follow standard canning process or store in refrigerator or freezer. (Contact your county extension office home economist or consult USDA bulletin #56 for complete and safe canning instructions.)

Makes 16 ounces

Cherry Marmalade

2 pounds sweet red or black cherries, pitted
4 cups sugar
Juice of 1/2 lemon
1/2 cinnamon stick per 8-ounce jar

Cut cherries in half; combine with the sugar and allow to macerate overnight.

Strain liquid into a large pot and bring to a boil; add lemon juice and boil 10 minutes. Add cherries and boil for 20 minutes. Add cinnamon sticks during last 5 minutes.

Pour cherries and syrup in sterilized jars, adding 1/2 cinnamon stick to each jar. Follow standard canning process or store in refrigerator or freezer. (Contact your county extension office home economist or consult USDA bulletin #56 for complete and safe canning instructions.)

Makes four 8-ounce jars.

Plum Jam

2 pounds ripe red, yellow or purple plums, pitted and quartered
Juice of 2 lemons
4 cups sugar

Combine ingredients in a deep pot. Bring to a rolling boil and lower the heat. Cook at medium heat 20 minutes, skimming the surface from time to time. Stir often until the mixture becomes transparent and very thick. The jam is done when the syrup leaves a heavy coating on a wooden spoon.

Push the entire mixture through a sieve and discard the skins. Follow standard canning process or store in refrigerator or freezer. (Contact your county extension office home economist or consult USDA bulletin #56 for complete and safe canning instructions.)

Makes one 16-ounce jar.

Variation: To make preserves, do not sieve the fruit.

Rose Petal Jam

1 pound fragrant, unsprayed red rose petals
Juice of 1 lemon
3 cups sugar
1/2 cup water
Juice of 3 lemons
1 cinnamon stick per jar

Place rose petals in a deep bowl; add lemon juice (1 lemon) and water to cover. Marinate until the water turns reddish.

Combine sugar and water in a saucepan. Bring to a boil and cook for 5 minutes. Drain rose petals and add. Bring to a boil again, and cook 20 minutes; add lemon juice and cook 5 minutes. Pour into sterilized jars. Add cinnamon sticks. Follow standard canning process or store in refrigerator or freezer. (Contact your county extension office home economist or consult USDA bulletin #56 for complete and safe canning instructions.)

Makes two 8-ounce jars.

Peach Apricot Jam

2 pounds peaches, pitted and sliced
2 pounds apricots, pitted and quartered
8 cups sugar
Juice of 1 lemon

Place all ingredients in a large pot and cook over medium heat until the mixture is very thick and the sugar becomes transparent, 20 to 30 minutes. Skim the surface from time to time as it cooks, and stir to prevent burning.

Remove from heat. Pour into hot sterilized jars. Follow standard canning process or store in refrigerator or freezer. (Contact your county extension office home economist or consult USDA bulletin #56 for complete and safe canning instructions.)

Makes two 16-ounce jars.

Passover Seder at the Behar's home. The Sultani, Pinhas, Benaroya, and Vaëna families. Geneva, 1949.

Passover Seder at the Pinhas home. The Sultani, Mizrachi, Behar, Vaëssa and Benaroya families. Geneva, 1950.

Grandmother and Grandfather.
Geneva, circa 1939.

Aunt Mimi takes me for a ride on the
Quai du Mont Blanc, 1948.

Passover Seder at Grandmother's. The Vaëna, Behar, Pinhas, Naftule, Sultani and
Benaroya families. Geneva, 1955.

Passover

A flurry of activity in the spring announced Passover's arrival. Everyone worked under pressure to prepare for this particular holiday because the Seder, the religious service, took place at home. Everyone joined forces to produce a uniquely Sephardic meal. And, as always, the cooking became a social occasion.

The matzah — the flat unleaven crackers symbolizing the haste with which the Israelites left Egypt — was baked in rounds to signify eternity. (I always ate my piece in a circle until it was gone.) My uncles made round matzah in the synagogue oven while the entire family scrubbed the kitchens until they shone and removed all food containing leaven, which was forbidden during the holiday. Even ordinary sugar was not allowed. We used solid, cone-shaped sugar which was broken off in pieces and crushed. We also put away our regular dishes, silverware, pots, pans, and other kitchen utensils and took out those that we used only for Passover.

As Grandmother prepared the lamb for baking, she told us that her parents roasted lamb outside in the garden when they lived in Turkey. The meat's aroma wafting through the kitchen made me impatient for the holiday, but I kept busy mixing the haroset, a rich paste made from nuts, wine, and spices that represents the mortar used by the Israelite slaves to build Egyptian cities.

As evening approached, Grandfather sent the oldest grandchild to the synagogue to find anyone who was alone. It was an obligation for the child to invite those who were alone to our Seder. At nightfall, we sat around the table listening to the story of the Israelites' escape from slavery, and singing Ladino songs that had Middle Eastern melodies. The Haggadah — a book explaining the exodus from Egypt and the Seder's rituals — was recited in Ladino the first night and in the language of the land on the second night. In Geneva, we recited it in French.

Our Passover customs fascinated me because they seemed unusual, yet sensible. One custom required the youngest child to hold the *afikoman,* a half piece of matzah wrapped in a white napkin, on his or her shoulder as a "burden." This kept the young child occupied throughout the long service. At the end of the service, Grandfather asked the child to return the afikoman and everyone ate a small piece.

When Grandfather recited the ten plagues that befell Egypt, he poured a little vinegar into a bowl of water, once for each plague, saying that the water diluted the effects of the plagues. He explained that only during Passover could a substance be added to water, a pure and sacred liquid. Water, however, could always be added to other substances.

But the most intriguing custom was the tradition of wearing grass hats and of covering the floor of the dining room with grass on the last day of Passover. The straw hats and grass symbolized the parting of the Red Sea which allowed the Hebrews to escape the Egyptian army. When the water parted, the reeds and grass at the sea's bottom were uncovered.

I remember wearing this hat and feeling very sentimental. Somehow I knew, even when I was very young, that our situation wasn't permanent. And I was right; in 1954 my family left Geneva for America. We were sponsored by Rabbi de Sola Pool from the Spanish and Portuguese Synagogue Shearith Israel in New York City. Here in America I renew my link with the past by creating a sumptuous feast for the family members who came with us.

The following dishes were served during Passover.

Haroset

1/2 cup raisins
1/2 cup dates
1/2 cup walnuts
1/2 cup almonds
2 cups apples
Juice of 1 orange
1/2 cup sweet wine
1/4 teaspoon cinnamon

Chop raisins, dates, walnuts, almonds, and apples fine but not mushy. Add orange juice, wine, and cinnamon. Mix well and let stand for several hours before serving, adding more wine if haroset becomes dry.

Makes 4 cups.

Hamindas (Brown Hard-Boiled Eggs)

6 eggs
3 tablespoons oil
Skins of 6 onions
1/8 teaspoon pepper

Place all ingredients in a saucepan, adding water to cover. Cover saucepan and simmer on very low heat for 8 hours, adding more water if necessary.

Serves 6.

Passover Potato Pancakes

3 potatoes, peeled and cut in quarters
2 eggs, beaten
Salt and pepper to taste
1 cup matzah meal
Peanut oil for frying

Boil potatoes in salted water; drain. Mash until smooth. Stir in egg, salt and pepper. Spoon by heaping tablespoons of potato mixture into the matzah meal; coat on both sides and flatten into patties. Fry in hot oil until golden on both sides.

Serves 4.

Poached Fish

1 onion sliced lengthwise to form crescents
1 carrot, cut into 1/4-inch slices
1 large bunch parsley, finely chopped (discard stems)
1/3 cup olive oil*
1 ripe tomato, cut into wedges
1 to 2 cups cold water
1 tablespoon vinegar
Juice of 1 lemon
Salt and pepper to taste
2 pounds carp fillets (or other white fish)

Sauté onions, carrots, and parsley in olive oil until onions are translucent. Add tomato and cook 5 minutes. Stir in water, vinegar, lemon, salt and pepper. Add the fish; cover and poach until opaque. Do not overcook. Place cooked fish and vegetables on a shallow serving platter.

Reduce sauce to 1 cup. Pour sauce over the fish and vegetables and refrigerate. The broth will solidify into an aspic. Serve cold in its gelatin with a light dusting of chopped parsley. Garnish with lemon slices.

Serves 6.

Poached Fish in Brown Butter and Parsley

2 pounds firm, white fish fillets
1/3 cup olive oil*
2 tablespoons vinegar
1 tablespoon salt
1/2 teaspoon pepper
8 ounces butter
1 large bunch parsley, finely chopped (discard stems)

Combine oil, vinegar, salt and pepper in a shallow frying pan. Place fish in pan and add water to barely cover. Poach gently until the fish is opaque. Do not overcook. Carefully remove the fish to a serving platter.

Brown butter; add parsley and stir. Spoon over the warm fish. Serve with lemon wedges.

Serves 4 to 6.

Baked Fish

2-pound fish fillet, thick
3 tablespoons olive oil*
1 large onion, chopped
2 cloves garlic, chopped
3 ripe tomatoes, peeled and chopped
4 tablespoons chopped parsley
4 tablespoons chopped dill weed
3 tablespoons lemon juice
Salt and pepper to taste

    Place fish in oiled baking pan. Sauté onions and garlic in olive oil until soft. Add remaining ingredients and cook until tomatoes are soft. Distribute sauce over fish and bake in a preheated 320° oven until fish flakes easily with a fork.
    Serves 4 to 6.

Baked Trout in Parsley and Tomatoes

4 whole, fresh water trout (about 3/4 pound each), or other white fish
1/3 cup olive oil*
2 large onions, chopped
1 large bunch parsley, chopped (discard stems)
1/2 teaspoon sugar
3 large ripe tomatoes, peeled and cut up
1/2 cup water
1/2 cup vinegar
Juice of 1 lemon

    Clean the trout. Wash and pat dry.
    Sauté onions and parsley in olive oil until onions are soft. Add sugar and tomatoes, and cook for 10 minutes. Add water, vinegar, and lemon juice and cook, stirring, 5 minutes more. Remove from heat.
    Arrange trout in an oiled baking pan. Pour the sauce over all and place in a preheated 450° oven. Bake, uncovered, 25 minutes or until tender.
    Serves 4.

* See note on page 169.

Cucumber and Chicken Soup

1/4 cup olive oil*
2 onions, chopped
2 pounds chicken, cut up
6 to 8 waxless cucumbers
Juice of 2 lemons
Salt and pepper to taste
2 large garlic cloves, chopped
1/2 cup chopped celery leaves
1/2 cup finely chopped parsley
1 teaspoon finely chopped dill weed

Sauté onions in oil; add chicken and sauté for 5 minutes, turning the pieces. Add water to cover; cover pan and simmer until chicken is almost tender.

Peel cucumbers, leaving 1/8 inch of cucumber pulp attached to peel. Cut peels into 1-inch pieces (save the pulp for salad).

Add the lemon juice, salt, pepper, garlic, and cucumber skins to the chicken. Simmer 10 to 15 minutes, then add the celery leaves, parsley and dill weed; simmer 5 minutes more. Serve with lemon wedges.

Serves 4 to 6.

Salata Egyptienne (Egyptian Salad)

2 each red, yellow and green bell peppers
4 medium onions
1/4 cup olive oil*
1 cup tomato juice
6 medium tomatoes, cut into wedges
1 teaspoon each salt and pepper
1/2 cup red wine vinegar

Remove seeds from bell peppers. Cut all vegetables lengthwise into 1/2 inch slices.

In a large frying pan, sauté the onions in olive oil until translucent, then add peppers and cook a few minutes more. Add tomato juice, cover, and cook on medium heat for 5 to 10 minutes. Add the tomatoes, salt and pepper; cover and cook 15 minutes longer. Add vinegar, cover, and cook another 10 to 15 minutes. Serve hot, cold, or at room temperature.

Serves 6 to 8.

Leeks and Carrots

1 bunch leeks
4 carrots, peeled and sliced in 1/4 inch rounds
Juice of 1 to 2 lemons, strained
Salt
2 tablespoons raw rice *
1/4 cup peanut or olive oil*
1/4 teaspoon sugar
2/3 cup water
6 tablespoons tomato sauce or chopped tomato

Cut off roots from bulb end of leeks. Remove tough outer leaves and trim tops. Slice lengthwise and wash thoroughly under running water. Cut into 1-inch pieces. Sauté carrots and rice in the oil for 5 minutes. Add remaining ingredients and cook, covered, on low-medium heat until tender. Refrigerate. Serve cold as an appetizer or a salad.
Serves 6.

Veal Heart in Wine Sauce

2 pounds veal heart, sliced into thin strips 1″long
1 cup dry red wine
1 tablespoon minced garlic
1 teaspoon dried rosemary
1/4 cup olive oil
3 medium onions, sliced lengthwise to form crescents
1 tablespoon flour
1 tablespoon vinegar
1/2 teaspoon each salt and pepper
1/2 cup chopped dill weed (or 2 Tbsp. dried)

Combine veal, wine, garlic, and rosemary. Marinate overnight in the refrigerator. The next day, drain into a bowl, adding flour to the marinade. Set aside.

Sauté sliced onions in olive oil. Add veal and cook 10 to 15 minutes until brown. Add marinade, vinegar, salt, pepper, and dill; cook 10 to 15 minutes to thicken sauce. Serve over rice. *
Serves 4 to 6.

* See note on page 169.

Roast Lamb Garni

1 lamb roast
3 cloves garlic, slivered (or more to taste)
Paprika
Oregano (may substitute dill or rosemary)
Salt and pepper
1/2 cup each vinegar and water, combined

For each person:
5 tiny, new potatoes, parboiled 10 minutes
1 green bell pepper, sliced lengthwise
1 ripe tomato, cut into wedges
1 onion, sliced lengthwise to form crescents

    Cut slits all over lamb and press a piece of garlic into each slit. Place lamb in a roasting pan, and arrange the vegetables around the lamb. Season with paprika, oregano, salt and pepper. Bake uncovered in a preheated 350° oven, basting every 15 minutes with vinegar-water mixture. Bake 15 to 20 minutes per pound, or test with a meat thermometer.

Fava Beans and Chicken

1/4 cup olive oil*
6 medium onions, sliced thickly
1 tablespoon finely chopped garlic
1 chicken, cut in serving pieces
1 pound fava beans (pods),* cut in thirds
Juice of 2 lemons

    Sauté onions and garlic in olive oil until soft. Add chicken and sauté until light brown. Add beans, lemon juice, and water to barely cover chicken. Cover and cook on low heat until chicken is tender.
    Serves 4 to 6.

    Note: Select young Fava beans. Pods should be soft, spongy with a thick velvety surface, and "seedless."

* See note on page 169.

Spinach Fritada

4 large eggs, beaten
2 sheets matzah, soaked in water, squeezed dry and crumbled
1 pound fresh spinach leaves, cooked, squeezed completely dry and chopped
2 cloves garlic, chopped very fine
1 teaspoon each salt and pepper, or to taste
Oil for frying

Combine all ingredients. Heat 1/4 inch of oil in a frying pan until very hot; lower heat to medium and add half the batter. Cook until the fritada is firm and set. Turn over (slide fritada onto a plate, invert frying pan over fritada, and turn both frying pan and plate over again) and fry the other side of the fritada. Transfer to a serving plate. Repeat with remaining batter.

To serve, stack one fritada over the other on the serving plate and slice in wedges.

Serves 2 to 4.

Variations: Substitute 3 cups zucchini grated on the large holes of a hand grater, or 3 cups chopped, cooked leeks for the spinach.

Passover Cheese and Spinach Fritadas

4 matzahs, broken into pieces and soaked in water
2 cups cooked, chopped spinach
4 eggs, beaten
1 cup grated Swiss Cheese
Salt and pepper to taste
Oil for frying

Drain matzahs and squeeze out excess water. Squeeze all liquid from spinach. Combine all ingredients and mix well. Drop by heaping tablespoons into hot oil and fry on both sides until light brown. Serve with tomato wedges.

Makes 12 small fritatas. Serves 6 to 8.

Variation: Divide batter into 2 equal portions and fry each as one large omelet. May substitute zucchini, yellow squash, or leeks for the spinach.

Romanian Passover Meat Pies

3 medium potatoes, boiled, peeled, and mashed
2 cups matzah cake meal
4 eggs, beaten
1/4 cup olive oil*
1 teaspoon each salt and pepper
Oil for deep frying

Filling
1/3 pound veal liver, thinly sliced
1/3 pound chicken livers
1/3 pound ground beef
Olive oil*
1 onion, very finely chopped
1 cup chopped parsley
1 clove garlic, pressed
1/2 teaspoon each salt and pepper
2 tablespoons matzah meal
2 eggs, beaten

With an electric mixer, beat potatoes, 1 cup matzah meal, eggs, olive oil, salt and pepper. Turn out onto a surface and knead remaining matzah meal into the dough for 15 minutes. Allow to rest 2 hours before using.

Make the filling: Broil veal liver and chicken livers. Sauté ground beef in olive oil, stirring constantly; remove to a colander. In the same pan, sauté onions until soft. Add parsley and cook 5 minutes more. Drain. Chop the livers in a grinder or food processor. Combine liver, ground beef, parsley, onions, garlic, salt, pepper, matzah meal, and eggs. Stir well.

Pinch off pieces of dough the size of an egg; roll out to a 4-inch diameter. Place 1 heaping teaspoon filling in the center; fold dough over the filling and pinch shut. Place a glass rim over each half moon and press down firmly to remove excess dough. Press and imprint all the way around the cut edge with the tines of a fork, to seal. Deep fry to golden brown.

Makes about 3 dozen.

* See note on page 169.

Passover Cheese Borekas

1 cup matzah cake meal
1 cup grated Swiss cheese
3 eggs, beaten
3 tablespoons peanut oil
3 tablespoons water
1/2 teaspoon salt
Oil for deep frying

Filling
1 cup grated Swiss Cheese
2 tablespoons potato starch
2 eggs, beaten
Salt and pepper

Combine matzah meal and cheese; add eggs, peanut oil, water, and salt. Blend together and allow to rest for 30 minutes at room temperature.

Make filling: combine cheese and potato starch, add remaining ingredients, and mix well.

Divide and shape the dough into balls the size of a large egg. Form a shell by pressing your thumb into the center of each ball. Enlarge the hollow and fill with a teaspoon of filling. Pinch the dough shut around the filling and gently reshape into a ball. Heat oil and deep fry until golden.

After all the dough balls have been filled and fried, bake in a preheated 350° oven for 20 minutes. Serve hot.

Makes about 12.

Fennel and Celeriac

2 celeriac roots, peeled and sliced in thin rounds
2 small or 1 large fennel, bulbous part, cut in thin slices
Juice of 1 lemon
1/4 cup olive oil*

Place vegetables in saucepan and barely cover with water. Add lemon juice and oil. Cook slowly, uncovered, until vegetables are tender and most of the water is absorbed. Stir gently from time to time. Serve cold or at room temperature, with remaining sauce.

Serves 6.

Leek and Potato Croquettes

3 cups cold mashed potatoes
1 onion, very finely chopped
1 tablespoon finely chopped garlic
3/4 cup matzah meal
4 large eggs, lightly beaten
5 tablespoons melted margarine
1/2 cup water
1 bunch leeks
Oil for frying

In a large bowl, combine potatoes, onion, garlic, matzah meal, eggs, margarine, and water. Stir well and set aside for 30 minutes.

Cut off roots from bulb end of leeks. Remove tough outer leaves and trim off tips. Slice lengthwise and wash thoroughly under running water. Cut into 1-inch pieces and parboil 5 minutes. Chop fine and add to the potato mixture; stir well.

Heat oil in a frying pan; add potato mixture in 2-inch dolops. Cook on both sides until brown and firm. Arrange on a dish and serve hot.

Makes 28.

Leek Croquettes

1 bunch leeks
1 pound grounded beef or lamb
3 eggs, beaten
1 teaspoon each salt and pepper, or to taste
Matzah meal
Peanut oil for frying

Cut off roots from bulb end of leeks. Remove tough outer leaves and trim off tops. Slice lengthwise and wash thoroughly under running water.

Chop leeks and cook in boiling salted water until tender, about 5 to 10 minutes. Squeeze out all excess water and mix together with meat, eggs, salt and pepper. Shape into finger rolls and roll in the matzah meal. Fry in oil until brown and cooked though.

Serves 6.

162

Potato Cakes

6 red potatoes, peeled
1 tablespoon salt
Peanut oil for frying
Pepper, optional

Grate potatoes and rinse in cold water. Drain thoroughly and stir in the salt. Place in a colander and let stand a minute or two. Divide into 6 equal portions and squeeze each until completely dry of all liquid.

Heat oil in a frying pan. Flatten grated potatoes into pancakes and gently slide them into the hot oil, one by one, making sure not to crowd them as they cook. Fry until golden on both sides. Drain. Serve immediately, seasoned with pepper.

Serves 4 to 6.

Celeriac and Carrots

2 celeriac roots, peeled
2 large carrots, peeled
Juice of 1 lemon
1 tablespoon white vinegar
1/4 cup olive oil*
Salt to taste
1/2 teaspoon sugar

Slice celeriac into 1/2 inch thick rounds; place in a bowl of water while slicing carrots 1/4 inch thick. Place all the ingredients in a saucepan and add water to barely cover. Cook slowly, uncovered, until the vegetables are tender. Serve at room temperature as an appetizer.

Serves 4.

* See note on page 169.

Fried Eggplant

1 medium eggplant, peeled
Salt
2 or 3 eggs, beaten
1 cup matzah meal
Peanut oil for frying

Cut eggplant diagonally into 1/4-inch slices. Salt on both sides and place on paper towels for 10 to 15 minutes. As the eggplant releases its water, change the paper towels.

Dip each slice in cold water and pat dry. Dip in beaten egg, then in matzah meal. Fry in medium-hot oil. Place on paper towels to drain. Serve immediately with lemon wedges.

Serves 4.

Variation: Before frying, dip the eggplant slices in matzah meal first then the eggs. You may substitute zucchini or yellow squash.

Passover Fried Cauliflower

1 head cauliflower, broken into florets
1 1/2 cups matzah meal
1/4 teaspoon each paprika, oregano, basil, marjoram, dill, chopped garlic,
    salt and pepper
3 eggs, beaten with 1/2 cup cool water
Olive oil* for frying

Mix matzah meal with seasonings.

Boil cauliflower until just done and slightly crisp. Drain. Dip cauliflower into egg-water mixture, roll in the matzah meal, and dip in egg again. Fry in 1/2 inch of olive oil until golden on all sides. Drain on paper towels and serve immediately.

Serves 6.

* See note on page 169.

Bimuellos

4 sheets matzah, broken
5 large eggs, beaten
3/4 cup raisins (optional)
3/4 cup walnuts, finely chopped (optional)
1 teaspoon cinnamon
2 teaspoons vanilla extract*
Peanut oil for frying
Sugar

Soak matzah in water and squeeze out excess water. Crumble into very small pieces and place in a large bowl. Add remaining ingredients and stir well.

Spoon heaping tablespoons of mixture into hot oil and flatten into patties as they fry. When patties are golden on both sides, remove and drain on paper towels. Arrange on an ovenproof serving dish and place in a warm oven for 10 minutes to dry. Dust with sugar and serve hot. Can be served at breakfast or for dessert.

Serves 6.

Melon Cream

4 pounds ripe cantaloupe or Persian melon
2 eggs
1/2 cup potato starch
1/2 cup sugar (scant)
1 teaspoon unflavored gelatin
1/2 teaspoon anise essential oil (optional)
2 teaspoons vanilla extract*

In a blender or food processor, purée half the cantaloupe; pour into a saucepan. Purée remaining cantaloupe with eggs, potato starch, sugar, and gelatin. Add to pan. Cook over low heat, stirring constantly, until mixture is very thick and coats the spoon. Add anise and stir again. Pour into individual cups and serve at room temperature.

Serves 6.

* See note on page 169.

Lemon Water Ices

1 1/2 cups sugar
3 cups water
5 lemons, grated zest and juice
2 egg whites

Combine sugar, water, and lemon juice in a saucepan, and boil 5 to 10 minutes to make a syrup; stir in the lemon zest. Place in freezer until almost frozen stirring several times to break up the forming ice crystals.

When the mixture is solidified but still easy to stir, remove from the freezer. Using an electric mixer, whip for about 2 minutes. Beat eggs whites to stiff peaks, and gently fold in, incorporating completely. Return to freezer until firm.

Beat again to a smooth light consistency. Place in a tightly-covered container and freeze until ice is very firm. Serve with cut-up fresh fruit.

Serves 6.

Cherries of Vijna Water Ices

3 cup black cherries, stems and pits removed
1 cup sugar
Juice of 1 lemon
Juice of 1 orange
2 eggs whites beaten to stiff peaks

Liquify the cherries in a food processor. Transfer the pulpy mixture to a deep pot and add sugar, lemon juice, and orange juice. Stir well and bring to a boil. Cook about 5 minutes, skimming the surface regularly with a large slotted spoon. Pour into a bowl and place in freezer until half-frozen. Stir periodically to break up forming ice.

When mixture is solidified but still easy to stir, remove from freezer and whip for about 2 minutes with electric mixer or food processor. Very gently fold in beaten egg whites, incorporating completely. Return mixture to freezer.

When firm, whip to a smooth light consistency. Transfer to a tightly covered container and freeze until very firm. To serve, scrape the surface of the frozen ice firmly with a large spoon and place in dessert cups. Top with a dolop of cherries of vijna (see recipe).

Serves 4 to 6.

Passover Loukoumades

1 cup water
1/2 cup oil
2 tablespoons sugar
1/8 teaspoon salt
1 cup matzah cake meal
4 large eggs
Peanut oil
Baklava syrup (see recipe)
Ground pistachios

Combine water, oil, sugar, and salt in a saucepan and bring to a boil. Add matzah meal all at one time. Beating all the while, continue to cook the dough until it pulls away from the sides of the pot and forms a large ball.

Remove from heat and continue mixing for 5 to 10 minutes to help the dough cool to lukewarm. Add eggs one at a time, beating thoroughly after each addition.

Drop by heaping teaspoonfuls into hot oil. They will submerge into the oil and then rise. Make sure that they fry on both side and have a uniform golden color. Dip in syrup and stack on a plate in the shape of a mountain. Sprinkle with ground pistachio nuts.

Makes about 2 dozen.

Note: May be made with flour at other times of the year.

Passover Almond Torte

6 large eggs, separated (room temperature)
Pinch salt
1 cup sugar
Grated zest of one lemon
10 ounces almond meal

With an electric mixer, beat egg whites and salt until foamy. Gradually add 1/2 cup sugar and whip until stiff satiny peaks form. Remove to another bowl. Whip egg yolks and remaining sugar until thick and pale yellow; add almond meal and mix thoroughly. Very gently fold egg whites into egg yolk mixture.

Pour into an ungreased 9-inch springform pan that is 3 inches deep. Bake in a preheated 300° oven for 40 minutes. Allow to cool completely before removing the sides of the springform pan and serving.

Serves 6 to 8.

Nut Cake

6 large eggs
2 cups sugar
Juice of 1 orange
1/2 cup peanut oil
1 teaspoon orange zest
1 teaspoon lemon zest
1/2 cup peanut oil
1 cup matzah cake meal
3 cups chopped walnuts

With an electric mixer, beat eggs and sugar until thick and lemony. Add orange juice, orange and lemon zest, and oil; mix well. Add cake meal and mix. Add walnuts and mix until well blended.

Pour into greased 13 x 9 cake pan and bake in a preheated 350° oven for 45 to 50 minutes or until top is golden brown. Allow to cool in the pan. Cut into squares to serve.

Serves 8 to 10.

Variation: Pour Baklava syrup (see recipe) over cake. Let stand for several hours. Serve with a dollop of yogurt on each serving, if desired.

Almond Macaroons

3 egg whites from large eggs
1 teaspoon vanilla extract*
3/4 cup sugar
16 ounces blanched almonds, finely ground (4 cups)
36 whole blanched almonds

In a double boiler, whip egg whites and sugar with a hand-held electric beater. Continue beating and cook gently until mixture thickens and forms soft shiny peaks. Remove from heat and continue to whip until cool and stiff. Gently fold in almond meal with a rubber spatula. Be sure almonds are well-distributed.

Drop by tablespoon onto oiled baking sheet. Gently press a whole almond into top of each. Bake in preheated 300° oven, 25 to 30 minutes for a chewy cookie, or 35 to 40 minutes for a crunchy cookie. Surface should be pale golden.

Makes 3 dozen.

Variation: Substitute walnut or hazelnut meal for the almonds.

* See note on page 169.

168

According to Sephardic practice, legumes such as beans and peas, and rice, may be served at Passover. This is different from the practice of Askenazi Jews, who are not permitted to eat these foods at Passover.

Olive oil and vanilla extract are acceptable if they are labeled "Kosher for Passover." You may substitute vegetable oil and orange juice, respectively. Kosher for Passover vanilla is available from Rokeach, in New Jersey (201-568-7750).

My family and I on board The Queen Mary, March 1954. On our way to America. Five days later we were in our new homeland, New York City, U.S.A. Later my mother changed her name to Dorothy. Her Americanization was complete.

Index

Candy(ies)
  almond milk for, 140
  halvah, 114
  Massapan (marzipan), 114
  walnut or almond, 112
Canella, 112
Cantaloupe. *see* Melon(s)
Cardamon
  in Turkish coffee, 117
Carp
  fillets in tomatoes and parsley, 98
  steaks, baked variation, 99
Carrot(s)
  artichokes and peas, 102
  celeriac, 163
  and leeks, 157
  pot roast and tomatoes with, 109
  and vinegar, glazed, 104
Cauliflower
  fried, 27, 164
    Passover, 164
  and potatoes
    dilled, 108
    with beef stew, 27
    with white sauce, 54
  souffle variation, 136
Celeriac
  carrots, 163
  and fennel, 161
Celery
  baked with cheese, variation, 53
  souffle variation, 136
Challah
  crowns, 123
  Sabbath, 97
Cheese
  and baked potato casserole, 55
  baked with celery variation, 53
  borekas
    Passover, 161
    variation, 124
  boyos, 31
  dill, 132
  and eggplant salad with garlic, 45
  endives baked with, 53
  filled coils, 86
  filling
    basic for filled breads, 122-123
    for borekitas, 138
  herbed, 133
  polenta with onions and, 23

and rice with scallions, 18
and spinach fritadas, Passover, 159
Cherry(ies)
  cold soup, 57
  fruit compote, 143
  fruit omelet, 135
  in Macedonian fruit salade, 61
  marmalade, 146
  preserved, 145
  sour
    cake, fresh, 79
    syrup, 115
  spiced, 61
  tart(s)
    with sweet cookie dough, 57
    with sweet yogurt dough, 60
  of Vijna
    syrup, 115
    water ices, 166
Chicken
  almond, 73
  boiled, 105
  Bulgarian, 104
  and fava beans, 158
  lemon, 103
  and lima beans, 103
  soups
    cucumber, 156
    lemon, 96
    lentil variation, 15
    pea and, 20
Chick pea(s)
  simmered, 25
  soup, 22
  in tomato sauce, 26
Cinnamon
  filling for tish pishti, 90, 91
  nut biscuits, 112
  in Turkish coffee, 117
Coffee, Turkish, 117
Cognac, in Turkish coffee, 117
Compote, fruit, 143

Cookie(s)
  almond
    butter, 77
    crisp, 77
    macaroons, 168
  anise biscotchos, 110
  dough for fruit tarts, 57
  fried pinwheels and bow ties, 111
  nut rolls, 87

175

Wine (*cont.*)
  tomato noodle soup variation, 24

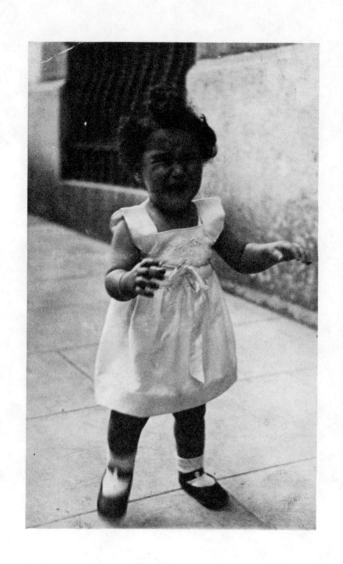

EXCELLENT COOKBOOKS FROM TRIAD

*THE CHOSEN — APPETIZERS & DESSERTS, by Marilyn Stone. Best recipes from 120 Jewish fund-raising cookbooks, tested and judged BEST! Kosher. "I love it!" (Maida Heatter). #101 PAPERBACK; #11X COMB BINDING.

*JEWISH COOKING MADE SLIM, by Majorie Weiner. Best recipes from fund-raising cookbooks are trimmed of calories by a Weight Watchers counselor. Kosher. "Delicious eating." (San Diego Union). # 187 PAPERBACK; #08X COMB BINDING.

*QUICK AND EASY, by Shelley Melvin. Fresh and from scratch — in 20 minutes or less! Includes regular and food processor instructions. Kosher. "Good food ... plenty of flavor ... always easy to make and serve." (Simone Beck) #551 PAPERBACK; #56X COMB BINDING.

FROM MY GRANDMOTHER'S KITCHEN — A SEPHARDIC COOKBOOK, By Viviane Miner with Linda Krinn. Family recipes handed down over generations, blending Turkish, Greek, Romanian and Bulgarian cuisines. Kosher. #233 PAPERBACK.

SOUPS OF HAKAFRI RESTAURANT, by Rena Franklin. A lifetime supply of delicious international soup recipes. "The most unusal cookbook of the year." (Los Angeles Herald Examiner) #128 HARDCOVER; #136 HARDCOVER, KOSHER EDITION.

CROSS CREEK KITCHENS, by Sally Morrison. Combine the "fresh-squeezed" taste of Florida with good, old-fashioned southern cooking. An American classic. Foreword by Governor and Mrs. Bob Graham. #063 PAPERBACK; #25X COMB BINDING; #500 DELUXE HARDCOVER.

*The Chosen series

- -

Use This Form To Order

Triad Publishing Company
1110 NW 8th Avenue, Dept. B
Gainesville, FL 32601
(904) 373-5308

☐ *Send information on fund-raising with Triad cookbooks.*

Qty.	Book	Price	Qty.	Book	Price
____	101	$ 8.95	____	233	$ 8.95
____	11X	11.95	____	128	12.95
____	187	8.95	____	136	12.95
____	08X	11.95	____	063	8.95
____	551	8.95	____	25X	11.95
____	56X	11.95	____	500	19.95

Name_____

Address_____

City_____ State_____ Zip_____

Please enclose $1.50 postage and handling. Florida resident add 5% sales tax.

Canadian residents use U.S. Dollar World Money Order
or check drawn on U.S. funds in U.S. Bank.